MERKABA: JOURNEY THROUGH SACRED GEOMETRY AND SPIRITUAL AWAKENING

Unveiling the Mystical Path of Chariot Mysticism

Holly Jane McConnell

S.D.N Publishing

CONTENTS

GENERAL DISCLAIMER

This book is intended to provide informative and educational material on the subject matter covered. The author(s), publisher, and any affiliated parties make no representations or warranties with respect to the accuracy, applicability, completeness, or suitability of the contents herein and specifically disclaim any implied warranties of merchantability or fitness for a particular purpose.

The information contained in this book is for general information purposes only and is not intended to serve as legal, medical, financial, or any other form of professional advice. Readers should consult with appropriate professionals before making any decisions based on the information provided. Neither the author(s) nor the publisher shall be held responsible or liable for any loss, damage, injury, claim, or otherwise, whether direct or indirect, consequential, or incidental, that may occur as a result of applying or misinterpreting the information in this book.

This book may contain references to third-party websites, products, or services. Such references do not constitute an endorsement or recommendation, and the author(s) and publisher are not responsible for any outcomes related to these third-party references.

In no event shall the author(s), publisher, or any affiliated parties be liable for any direct, indirect, punitive, special, incidental, or other consequential damages arising directly or indirectly from any use of this material, which is provided "as is," and without warranties of any kind, express or implied.

By reading this book, you acknowledge and agree that you assume all risks and responsibilities concerning the applicability and consequences of the information provided. You also agree to indemnify, defend, and hold harmless the author(s), publisher, and any affiliated parties from any and all liabilities, claims, demands, actions, and causes of action whatsoever, whether or not foreseeable, that may arise from using or misusing the information contained in this book.

Although every effort has been made to ensure the accuracy of the information in this book as of the date of publication, the landscape of the subject matter covered is continuously evolving. Therefore, the author(s) and publisher expressly disclaim responsibility for any errors or omissions and reserve the right to update, alter, or revise the content without prior notice.

By continuing to read this book, you agree to be bound by the terms and conditions stated in this disclaimer. If you do not agree with these terms, it is your responsibility to discontinue use of this book immediately.

INTRODUCTION
TO MERKABA

UNDERSTANDING MERKABA: ORIGINS AND EVOLUTION

The Merkaba, a concept steeped in antiquity, mysticism, and spiritual symbolism, traces its roots back to ancient texts and practices. Its origins are interwoven with the fabric of early Jewish mysticism, particularly during the period of Merkabah mysticism, which thrived from approximately 100 BCE to 1000 CE. This mystical tradition, deeply rooted in Jewish esotericism, revolved around visions of a divine chariot, or Merkaba, as detailed in the visions of prophets like Ezekiel.

Early Jewish Merkabah Mysticism

Jewish mysticism, or Kabbalah, encompasses a broad spectrum of mystical practices and interpretations. Early on, it was profoundly influenced by prophetic visions, like those of Ezekiel and Isaiah, which described complex, often cryptic images of the divine throne or chariot. These visions formed the bedrock of Merkabah mysticism, a tradition that spanned several centuries and evolved through various forms. The central theme of this tradition was the quest to understand and experience the divine presence, often visualized as a celestial chariot or Merkaba.

The Merkaba in Rabbinic Literature

Merkabah mysticism, while rooted in ancient prophetic visions, found its expression in rabbinic literature through both direct and indirect references. The Talmud, a central text in Rabbinic Judaism, occasionally mentions the Merkaba but shrouds it in mystery and reverence. Rabbinic commentaries on the Merkaba stressed the importance of this concept, yet they also highlighted the dangers of delving too deeply into its secrets. This notion of caution and reverence underscores the sacredness and power attributed to the Merkaba in Jewish mysticism.

Merkaba: Beyond Jewish Mysticism

The concept of the Merkaba transcends its origins in Jewish mysticism, embodying universal themes found in various spiritual practices. It's often represented by the interlocking tetrahedrons, symbolizing the balance and unity of different aspects of existence, like masculine and feminine  energies or earthly and divine realms. This geometric representation is not just a static symbol; it's envisioned as a dynamic, spinning structure that facilitates energy flow and connection with higher consciousness.

Merkaba in Meditation and Spiritual Practices

In contemporary spiritual practices, the Merkaba symbol plays a central role in meditation, energy healing, and chakra balancing. Practitioners focus on the symbol to align their energies, achieve deep relaxation, and attain heightened awareness. The Merkaba is also believed to play a crucial role in astral travel and accessing higher realms of consciousness. It serves as a bridge between the physical and spiritual, enabling individuals to tap into their inner power and expand their awareness.

INTRODUCION TO MERKABA

The Merkaba's Healing Properties

Apart from its role in meditation and spiritual exploration, the Merkaba is also revered for its healing properties. It's believed to balance and align the chakras, cleanse negative energy, and promote emotional well-being. By engaging with the Merkaba, individuals can experience spiritual growth, transformation, and a deeper connection with the divine. It's a symbol that not only represents spiritual concepts but also actively participates in the individual's journey towards enlightenment and self-realization.

The Merkaba, from its ancient roots in Jewish mysticism to its modern applications in spiritual practices, represents a journey of understanding and connecting with the divine. It encapsulates a myriad of meanings, from a celestial chariot in prophetic visions to a symbolic representation of energy and consciousness in current spiritual practices. As a sacred geometric form, it continues to inspire, heal, and guide individuals on their spiritual paths, transcending cultural and temporal boundaries to maintain its relevance and power in contemporary spirituality.

MERKABA IN ANCIENT TEXTS

The Merkaba, an enigmatic symbol in Jewish mysticism, possesses profound historical and spiritual significance. Its presence in ancient texts reflects a complex intertwining of mysticism, theology, and philosophy. Let's delve into the historical accounts and interpretations of the Merkaba, exploring its deep roots in early Jewish mysticism and its evolution through various cultural and religious lenses.

Merkaba in Jewish Mysticism

In Jewish mysticism, particularly in Merkabah mysticism, the Merkaba symbolizes the divine chariot, as described in the visions of prophets like Ezekiel. The earliest Rabbinic Merkabah commentaries, dating from around the first to the second century CE, provide exegetical expositions of these prophetic visions. These interpretations often focus on the divine throne and its surrounding celestial beings, reflecting a deep contemplation of God's presence in the heavens.

Symbolism and Meaning in Merkabah Literature

The term 'Merkaba' combines three words: 'mer' (light), 'ka' (spirit), and 'ba' (body), signifying the union of spirit and body surrounded by light. This sacred symbol, found extensively in Merkabah literature, is portrayed as two interlocking tetrahedrons spinning in opposite directions. This creates a dynamic energy field, believed to be present around every person, symbolizing the union of opposing energies: feminine and masculine, earthly and divine.

The Merkaba in Hekhalot Literature

Hekhalot literature, a significant component of Merkabah mysticism, comprises mystical texts that detail ascents into the divine palaces and visions of the heavenly throne. Originating after the destruction of the Second Temple in 70 CE, this literature represents a spiritualization of the pilgrimages to the earthly temple that were no longer possible. These texts focus on mystical journeys to the heavenly abode, divine visions, and interactions with angels, aiming to gain deeper insight into the Torah and the divine realm.

The Merkaba in the Context of Religious Dynamics

Historians often debate whether the Merkaba's ascent and unitive themes emerged from external influences, such as Gnostic thought, or as a natural progression within Rabbinic Judaism. The Merkaba's depiction in religious texts and its interpretation by figures like Maimonides in the 12th century suggest a deep-rooted connection to Jewish religious thought, expanding beyond simple mythological representation.

The Merkaba in Ritual and Meditation

Beyond its mystical interpretations, the Merkaba also finds practical applications in rituals and meditation. In rituals, the Merkaba is used to create a sacred space, often involving visualization techniques to feel its energy and connect with higher guidance. In meditation, the Merkaba serves as a tool for enlightenment and spiritual empowerment, enabling individuals to connect with their inner selves and higher realms.

The Merkaba's Role in Spiritual Growth

The Merkaba's rich history and varied uses highlight its role in facilitating spiritual growth and connection. It's a symbol that encourages individuals to contemplate their place in the world and the nature of their existence. In Hasidic philosophy, the Merkaba is seen as a multi-

layered analogy that provides insight into the nature of humanity and the world, teaching us to become better individuals by understanding the harmony of opposing forces.

The Merkaba's presence in ancient religious and mystical texts underscores its significance across various spiritual traditions. It's a symbol that has captivated mystics and seekers, offering a window into understanding the divine and the deeper aspects of our existence. As a sacred vehicle, the Merkaba not only represents spiritual concepts but also actively participates in an individual's journey towards enlightenment and self-realization.

THE GEOMETRY OF MERKABA AND ITS SYMBOLIC SIGNIFICANCE

The Merkaba, a symbol deeply embedded in spiritual and esoteric traditions, represents a complex interplay of geometry and metaphysics. Its structure, comprising two interlocking tetrahedrons, holds profound symbolic meanings, encapsulating the unity of opposites and the connection between the physical and spiritual realms. Let's explore the geometrical structure of the Merkaba, delving into its symbolic significance and applications in various spiritual practices.

The Star Tetrahedron Structure

At its core, the Merkaba is symbolized by the star tetrahedron, a three-dimensional figure formed by two intersecting tetrahedra spinning in opposite directions. This structure symbolizes numerous binary relationships fundamental to human and cosmic existence. It represents the interplay of male and female energies, the convergence of spiritual and physical dimensions, and the balance between earth and sky. The upward-pointing tetrahedron is often linked to the divine, masculine, and celestial realms, while the downward-pointing tetrahedron aligns with the earthly, feminine, and material aspects of existence.

Symbolism and Spiritual Interpretation

In Jewish mysticism, particularly in Merkabah tradition, the Merkaba serves as a metaphysical construct for contemplating heavenly mysteries and the divine nature. Ezekiel's vision of God's chariot, detailed with symbolic elements, forms the basis of Merkabah mysticism. This intricate structure is seen as a coded language representing aspects of the divine system and creation process. The Merkaba's significance extends beyond a vehicle in Ezekiel's vision; it symbolizes the divine presence and the complex relationship between the divine and the earthly realms.

Merkaba in Esoteric Teachings

In esoteric teachings, the Merkaba transcends its symbolic representation, becoming a tool for spiritual practice. It is believed that by visualizing and activating the Merkaba, one can achieve higher states of consciousness and even travel across different dimensions. This practice involves complex meditation techniques that align the individual's energy fields and chakras, facilitating spiritual awakening and enlightenment.

Sacred Geometry and the Merkaba

The star tetrahedron of the Merkaba is closely associated with sacred geometry, which attributes symbolic meanings to certain geometric shapes. This field of study explores the hidden patterns in nature, art, and architecture, revealing the fundamental structures of the universe and the order within creation. The Merkaba, in this context, transcends its mystical origins, finding relevance in metaphysics, cosmology, and quantum physics.

Practical Applications of the Merkaba

The Merkaba finds practical applications in meditation, energy healing, and chakra balancing. It enhances spiritual practices by aligning energies, achieving deep relaxation, and facilitating heightened awareness. Additionally, the Merkaba is used for astral travel and accessing higher consciousness, believed to connect individuals with wisdom and guidance from higher realms.

Merkaba's Healing Properties

The Merkaba is also revered for its healing properties. It aids in balancing and aligning chakras, clearing negative energy, and promoting emotional well-being. By engaging with the Merkaba, individuals experience spiritual growth, transformation, and a deeper connection with the divine. The incorporation of crystals, such as amethyst and clear quartz, amplifies the healing effects of the Merkaba, enhancing meditation sessions and providing continuous support.

The geometrical structure of the Merkaba, with its deep-rooted symbolic significance, offers a multifaceted perspective on spirituality and metaphysics. It serves as a potent emblem of the journey towards spiritual growth, inner harmony, and the unification of disparate aspects of existence. The Merkaba's presence in various spiritual traditions underscores its universal appeal and enduring relevance in the quest for spiritual enlightenment.

THEORETICAL
FOUNDATIONS

SACRED GEOMETRY AND SPIRITUAL SYMBOLS

Sacred geometry, an ancient science and art form, holds significant power in spiritual symbolism and practices. It is deeply interconnected with the Merkaba, a symbol of immense spiritual importance. Let's explore how sacred geometry, particularly the Merkaba, plays a pivotal role in spiritual awakening and practices.

The Essence of Sacred Geometry

Sacred geometry refers to geometric patterns and shapes that recur in nature and are used in various cultural and religious contexts. These shapes and patterns are seen as manifestations of the fundamental structures of our universe and the hidden order within creation. Sacred geometry posits that certain geometric shapes and proportions contain sacred or spiritual significance, transcending physical properties.

Merkaba: A Confluence of Geometry and Spirituality

The Merkaba, a key figure in sacred geometry, is a three-dimensional star formed by two intersecting tetrahedrons. This structure, often referred to as the Star Tetrahedron, symbolizes the union of opposing energies and serves as a visual representation of spiritual ascension and the connection between divine and earthly realms.

Interlocking Tetrahedrons: Symbolizing Balance and Harmony

The Merkaba's interlocking tetrahedrons are associated with balance, harmony, and unity between different aspects of existence, such as masculine and feminine energies and the earthly and divine realms. This structure facilitates energy flow and aids in connecting with higher consciousness, making it a potent symbol in various spiritual practices.

Merkaba in Meditation and Healing

Merkaba meditation is a practice involving visualization or chanting to activate personal Merkabas. It is believed to tap into inner power, expand awareness, and align with higher purpose. Practitioners utilize the Merkaba symbol during meditation to align energies, achieve deep relaxation, and attain heightened awareness. Additionally, the Merkaba is used in chakra balancing, as each point of the star corresponds to one of the seven main chakras.

Facilitating Astral Travel and Higher Consciousness

Some individuals use the Merkaba for astral travel or out-of-body experiences during deep meditation states. It is viewed as a gateway to higher consciousness or spiritual realms, providing access to wisdom and guidance from higher beings or dimensions.

The Merkaba's Healing Properties

The Merkaba possesses powerful healing properties. It aids in balancing and aligning chakras, clearing negative energy, and promoting emotional well-being. Engaging with the Merkaba symbol can activate dormant energies, opening doors to higher consciousness and expanded awareness. It serves as a tool for connecting with higher realms and divine guidance.

Amplifying Healing with Crystals

To enhance the healing effects of the Merkaba, many practitioners incorporate crystals into their practice. Crystals like amethyst and clear quartz, known for their unique energetic properties, are used alongside the Merkaba symbol to amplify meditation sessions or as jewelry for continuous support.

Merkaba: A Divine Vehicle

In Jewish culture and religion, the Merkaba is seen as a multi-layered approach to understanding the world, the ecosystem, and human nature. It is viewed as a divine vehicle made of light, designed to connect or transport the body and spirit to higher realms.

The sacred geometry of the Merkaba, with its profound spiritual symbolism, offers a multi-dimensional understanding of reality. It represents a journey towards spiritual growth, inner harmony, and the unification of different aspects of existence. The Merkaba's role in meditation, healing, and astral travel highlights its significance in enhancing spiritual practices and personal growth.

EZEKIEL'S CHARIOT AND MERKABA MYSTICISM

Ezekiel's Chariot, a profound mystical vision from the Book of Ezekiel, is a cornerstone of Jewish Merkaba mysticism. Let's delve into the analysis and interpretation of this vision and its significant role in the development of Merkaba mysticism.

The Vision of Ezekiel

Ezekiel's vision, as described in the opening of his biblical book, presents a complex tableau of a divine chariot, surrounded by four winged creatures, and enveloped in fire. This vision marks the beginning of Merkaba or Chariot mysticism, a mystical tradition within Judaism that strives to recreate and understand this prophetic experience. Ezekiel's encounter, depicting a heavenly chariot and its awe-inspiring details, has been the subject of extensive mystical and theological speculation.

Merkaba Mysticism: An Overview

Merkaba mysticism, originating around the second century CE, focuses on the pursuit of divine visions and ascents to heavenly realms. It represents a specific strain of Jewish mysticism that emphasizes ecstatic and visionary experiences. The term 'Merkaba' itself is derived from the Hebrew word for 'chariot,' symbolizing the throne-chariot of God.

The Mystical Journey and Ascension

Merkaba mystics aim to re-enact Ezekiel's visionary ascent to explore the heavens and encounter the Divine. This journey is described in Heikhalot literature, which contains vivid and imaginative descriptions of God's heavenly domain. These texts offer a guide to mystical travels into the

palaces housing the Divine Throne, portraying the journey through heavenly precincts and encounters with celestial beings.

Symbolism in Ezekiel's Vision

The vision includes winged creatures with hybrid features and wheels within wheels, symbolizing the ability to move in any direction. These elements represent the complexity of the divine chariot and the intricate nature of the heavenly domain. Ezekiel's description transcends earthly understanding, depicting a vibrant heavenly reality with a deep spiritual significance.

Rabbinic Commentary and Interpretation

Rabbinic literature, such as the Talmud and Midrash, also contains discussions on the Merkaba, although these are less esoteric compared to Heikhalot literature. These texts reveal how the vision of the divine throne is accessible through the study of Torah and Talmud, leading to mystical experiences of the divine realm.

The Role of Merkaba in Spiritual Practices

Merkaba mysticism is not just about intellectual contemplation; it involves practical techniques for spiritual ascent. This includes visualization, meditation, and specific rituals aimed at replicating the prophet's experience. The Merkaba serves as a vehicle for spiritual transformation, guiding practitioners towards higher consciousness.

The Influence of Merkaba Mysticism

Merkaba mysticism has had a profound influence on various forms of Jewish spirituality, including Kabbalistic thought. It represents a unique approach to understanding the divine and the universe, blending mystical vision with theological inquiry.

Ezekiel's Chariot and Merkaba mysticism present a rich tapestry of spiritual exploration, blending visionary experiences with theological insights. This mystical tradition has deeply influenced Jewish thought, offering pathways to spiritual ascension and a deeper understanding of the divine.

MERKABA IN KABBALISTIC THOUGHT

Merkaba mysticism and Kabbalistic thought are deeply intertwined, revealing a rich tapestry of Jewish mystical tradition. Let's explore the place of Merkaba within Kabbalistic thought, exploring its significance and interpretations.

The Integration of Merkaba and Kabbalah

Kabbalah, a form of Jewish mysticism, has incorporated Merkaba mysticism since its early development. Merkaba, meaning 'chariot', is rooted in the visionary traditions of early Jewish mystics, particularly those focused on the prophetic visions of Ezekiel's chariot. Kabbalistic thought expanded on these visions, integrating them with its own mystical explorations of the nature of God, the universe, and the human soul.

The Zohar and Merkaba Mysticism

The Zohar, a foundational work of Kabbalah, contains numerous references to Merkaba mysticism. It provides a complex interpretation of Ezekiel's vision, using it as a framework to discuss the nature of God, the structure of the cosmos, and the path to spiritual ascension. The Zohar's interpretation of Merkaba is both symbolic and metaphysical, offering a deeper understanding of the divine chariot as a representation of God's presence and a vehicle for spiritual journey.

The Sefirot and the Merkaba

In Kabbalistic thought, the Sefirot – the ten attributes through which the divine manifests – are often associated with the structure of the Merkaba. This association presents the Merkaba as not just a static symbol, but a dynamic representation of the divine energies and processes. The interplay of these energies mirrors the mystical journey of the soul towards spiritual enlightenment.

The Heikhalot Literature

Heikhalot literature, closely associated with Merkaba mysticism, describes mystical ascents into heavenly realms. These texts are considered by some to be precursors to Kabbalistic literature. They focus on the practitioner's journey through various heavenly palaces, each representing different aspects of the divine and spiritual realization.

Mystical Experiences and Practices

Merkaba mysticism in Kabbalah encourages the pursuit of direct, personal experiences of the divine. This involves complex meditative practices, visualizations, and ethical preparations, aiming to replicate the prophetic experiences of figures like Ezekiel and Enoch.

Contemplative and Practical Aspects

Kabbalistic study of the Merkaba combines contemplative and practical aspects. It's not just about understanding the metaphysical structure of the divine chariot but also about applying this understanding to enhance spiritual growth, ethical behavior, and connection to God.

Merkaba and Tikkun Olam

In Kabbalah, the concept of Tikkun Olam – repairing the world – is often linked with Merkaba mysticism. The Merkaba symbolizes the alignment of the human with the divine, encouraging actions that bring about spiritual and physical harmony in the world.

Merkaba's place in Kabbalistic thought is profound, offering a bridge between ancient mystical traditions and contemporary spiritual practices. It represents a journey towards understanding the divine, the universe, and our place within it, integrating profound mystical visions with practical spiritual pursuits.

MERKABA AND
CONSCIOUSNESS

ACCESSING HIGHER CONSCIOUSNESS

In exploring the profound connection between Merkaba and consciousness, we delve into how this ancient symbol serves as a key to unlocking higher states of awareness. The Merkaba, derived from the Egyptian words 'Mer' (Light), 'Ka' (Spirit), and 'Ba' (Body), represents a field of energy shaped like a star tetrahedron that surrounds the body. This energetic field is a gateway to spiritual ascension, facilitating a deep connection with the higher realms.

Merkaba: A Vehicle for Higher Consciousness

The Merkaba is often visualized as a conduit to higher planes of existence. It enables practitioners to transcend the physical boundaries of their consciousness and tap into a universal wisdom. This sacred geometry is not just a symbol; it's an active tool for spiritual growth and enlightenment, offering guidance and insights from higher dimensions.

Enhancing Self-Awareness

Engaging with the Merkaba significantly heightens self-awareness. It creates a reflective mirror for one's thoughts, emotions, and actions, fostering a deeper understanding of the self. This enhanced awareness is pivotal for personal evolution, facilitating choices that are more aligned with one's authentic desires and aspirations.

Intuition and the Third Eye Chakra

The Merkaba is intricately linked with the third eye chakra, the center of intuition in the human energy system. Regular interaction with the Merkaba sharpens intuitive faculties, making them more profound and accessible. This heightened intuition acts as an inner compass, aiding in decision-making and providing clarity in complex situations.

Protective Energetic Field

Beyond its role in consciousness elevation, the Merkaba acts as a protective shield. It safeguards individuals from adverse energies and external influences that can disrupt emotional and spiritual equilibrium. This protection is crucial for maintaining a balanced and harmonious existence.

Techniques of Merkaba Meditation

Merkaba meditation is a methodical process aimed at activating this energy field. It encompasses distinct breathing patterns and focused visualization. The meditation begins in a tranquil setting, progressing through breaths associated with various chakras. The visualization of the Merkaba field spinning around the body is central to this practice. The culmination of this meditation is achieving a high-frequency spin of the energy field, aligning it with the speed of light, a state indicative of accessing higher consciousness and spiritual awakening.

The Role of Breath in Merkaba Activation

Breathing patterns in Merkaba meditation are crucial for its effectiveness. The rhythmic inhalation and exhalation facilitate the alignment of the human energy field with the universe's vibrational frequency. These breathing techniques are not just physical exercises; they are spiritual tools that harmonize the body's energy with cosmic energy.

Visualization: The Heart of Merkaba Practice

Visualization in Merkaba meditation involves imagining the intersecting tetrahedrons surrounding the body. This mental construction of the Merkaba is vital for inviting positive energy and elevating awareness. Practitioners focus on the concepts of light, spirit, and body, each represented in the Merkaba, to deepen their meditation experience.

Connecting with Higher Consciousness

The primary goal of Merkaba meditation is to establish a connection with higher consciousness. This practice is a journey toward spiritual enlightenment, where practitioners remain open to receiving divine guidance and insights. Trust and openness are key as one navigates this path to elevated awareness.

Hand Positions and Movements

Merkaba meditation also involves specific hand positions and movements. These gestures are not mere physical actions but are symbolic of grounding energy and focusing the mind. Maintaining these hand positions throughout the meditation aids in harnessing the full potential of the Merkaba energy field.

Accessing higher consciousness through Merkaba involves a combination of visualization, breathwork, and a deep understanding of the symbol's sacred geometry. This practice is a transformative journey, elevating practitioners to a realm of heightened awareness and spiritual connection.

MERKABA AND
THE CHAKRAS

The Interconnection of Merkaba and Chakras

Merkaba, a term derived from ancient Egyptian words 'Mer' (light), 'Ka' (spirit), and 'Ba' (body), represents the integration of spirit and body enveloped in light. The chakras, central to many spiritual practices, are energy centers within the body that regulate various aspects of our physical, emotional, and spiritual well-being. Merkaba, with its sacred geometry, plays a crucial role in balancing and aligning these chakras, facilitating an enhanced state of consciousness and holistic health.

Geometric Structure and Chakra Alignment

The Merkaba comprises two interlocking tetrahedrons, forming a star-like pattern often associated with the Star of David. This structure is key to understanding Merkaba's influence on the chakras. Each point of the star corresponds to a chakra, providing a direct connection for energy alignment and balance. Regular meditation and visualization of the Merkaba can lead to the activation and harmonization of the chakra system.

Meditation and Chakra Activation

Merkaba meditation techniques involve deep breathwork and visualization of the spinning tetrahedrons. This practice serves to activate the chakras, enhance the flow of life force energy (prana), and cleanse negative energies. Practitioners visualize a vertical tube along the spine, connecting the chakras, and imagine prana flowing through, revitalizing each energy center. This alignment fosters emotional stability, mental clarity, and heightened intuition.

Balancing Masculine and Feminine Energies

The two tetrahedrons of the Merkaba represent the masculine and feminine energies within us, symbolizing action and receptivity, strength and nurturing. Their interlocking nature in Merkaba meditation fosters a balance between these energies, essential for personal growth and spiritual advancement.

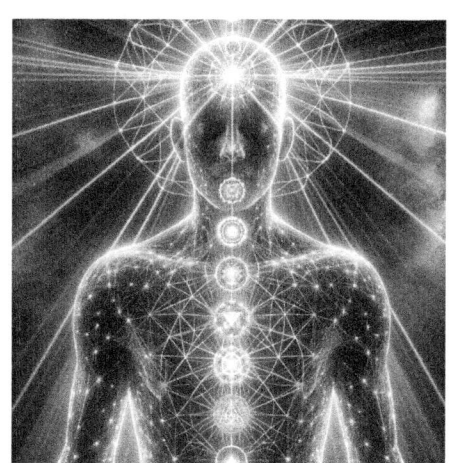

Healing and Transformation

The Merkaba chakra's role in healing transcends physical well-being, encompassing emotional and mental health. It aids in releasing emotional blockages, enhancing emotional stability, and promoting mental well-being. This transformation is not just limited to the individual but also influences the collective consciousness, contributing to a harmonious and balanced existence.

Spiritual Awakening

Engaging with the Merkaba chakra is a journey towards spiritual awakening. It opens the gateway to higher consciousness, allowing practitioners to connect with their higher selves and the divine. This awakening brings about profound insights, enhances self-awareness, and unlocks spiritual gifts and potential.

Practical Applications

Incorporating the Merkaba chakra in various practices like meditation, energy healing, and intention setting amplifies their efficacy. It becomes a tool for personal transformation, spiritual growth, and the manifestation of desires. The Merkaba's protective powers also play a role in chakra cleansing, ensuring a free flow of energy across all chakras.

Merkaba in Daily Life

Integrating Merkaba into daily life involves mindfulness and conscious living. By being aware of the Merkaba's influence on the chakras, individuals can maintain a balanced state of being, nurture their spiritual growth, and manifest a harmonious reality. This integration leads to a life filled with joy, love, and spiritual fulfillment.

The relationship between Merkaba and the chakras is profound, offering pathways to holistic health, spiritual awakening, and transformation. By understanding and actively working with this connection, individuals can achieve a state of balance and harmony, both within themselves and in their interactions with the world.

MERKABA AND THE HUMAN ENERGY FIELD

The Essence of the Merkaba in Energy Fields

The Merkaba, symbolizing light, spirit, and body, forms an energy field around the human body, representing the integration of these elements. This field, structured as two interlocking tetrahedrons, is a living energy form, extending and interacting with the universe's energy matrix. The Merkaba is essentially the human light vehicle, facilitating travel through dimensions and serving as a bridge between physical and spiritual realms.

Activation and Interaction with the Energy Field

Activating the Merkaba involves a series of breathwork and visualization techniques, where the practitioner visualizes the Merkaba spinning around their body. This spinning is crucial for aligning with Source energy and enabling the energy field to function as a protective, healing, and consciousness-expanding tool. The activation process requires personal intention and a commitment to spiritual development.

Merkaba: A Pathway to Higher Consciousness

The Merkaba is seen as a gateway to higher consciousness. By working with this sacred geometry, individuals can access wisdom and guidance from higher dimensions, enhance self-awareness, and develop a more profound understanding of the self. This path leads to an expanded intuition, allowing for better decision-making and life navigation.

The Protective Qualities of the Merkaba

As an energetic shield, the Merkaba protects against negative influences, maintaining energetic boundaries and contributing to a sense of balance and well-being. This protective aspect is integral to its role in clearing negative energy and promoting emotional health.

Merkaba and Chakra Alignment

The Merkaba aids in balancing and aligning the chakras, the body's energy centers. This alignment fosters physical, emotional, and spiritual vitality, harmonizing the individual's overall energy system.

Merkaba in Meditation and Spiritual Practices

Incorporating the Merkaba into meditation and spiritual practices amplifies their benefits. This integration enhances spiritual growth, facilitates astral travel, and connects practitioners with their higher selves. The Merkaba also plays a role in clearing chakra blockages and promoting energetic flow.

Mantras and Sacred Geometry in Merkaba Activation

Mantras and sacred geometry are valuable tools in activating the Merkaba. They align energy with specific vibrational patterns and stimulate the energetic system, enhancing the connection with higher dimensions and fostering spiritual development.

The Merkaba's Role in Personal Growth

The Merkaba is not only a tool for spiritual ascension but also for personal growth and healing. By working with the Merkaba, individuals can confront and integrate unresolved traumas, foster mental clarity, and achieve emotional release.

Expanding Psychic Abilities and Intuition

Awakening the Merkaba enhances psychic abilities and intuition. As practitioners tap into higher states of consciousness, they gain access to knowledge beyond ordinary perception, deepening their understanding of themselves and the universe.

The Merkaba, as a multidimensional energy structure, plays a crucial role in human spiritual and personal development. By understanding and activating this energy field, individuals can embark on a transformative journey, exploring the depths of their consciousness and unlocking their full potential.

PRACTICAL
APPLICATIONS

MERKABA IN MEDITATION AND MINDFULNESS

Understanding Merkaba Meditation

Merkaba meditation is an ancient practice deeply rooted in sacred geometry and spiritual symbolism. The term "Merkaba" itself derives from the Egyptian words for light (Mer), spirit (Ka), and body (Ba), symbolizing the harmonious activation of these aspects. The meditation focuses on an electro-magnetic field, shaped in the form of two interlocking tetrahedrons that surround the body, and is associated with sacred geometry. This field is believed to extend through all dimensions and universes.

The Activation of Merkaba

Activation of the Merkaba is a profound experience, traditionally achieved by drawing and meditating on the mandalas of the Flower of Life. The process involves visualizing the sacred geometric shapes and using specific breathwork techniques. This meditation purifies the flow of prana (life force) through the body and mind, harmonizes brain hemispheres, and opens the third eye pineal gland.

Merkaba Meditation Techniques

1. **Preparation and Breathing**: Begin by sitting comfortably and engaging in mindful breathing to calm and clear the mind.

2. **Visualization of Tetrahedrons**: Visualize two tetrahedrons - one above and one below the body, interconnected and encompassing the body. This visual representation is crucial for the activation process.

3. **Breathwork**: Engage in a series of breaths, with each breath focusing on different chakras, visualizing the infusion of light and energy from these chakras into the tetrahedrons.

4. **Activation of Merkaba**: The culmination of the meditation involves visualizing the tetrahedrons spinning and the energy field around the body expanding and activating the Merkaba.

Benefits of Merkaba Meditation

1. **Enhanced Self-Awareness and Emotional Well-Being**: Merkaba meditation fosters self-awareness, helping practitioners become more attuned to their thoughts, emotions, and actions.

2. **Elevated Consciousness**: Regular practice can lead to a heightened sense of consciousness and connection to the divine.

3. **Energetic Protection**: The activated Merkaba field acts as a shield, protecting against negative energies and maintaining energetic boundaries.

Integrating Merkaba in Mindfulness Practices

Merkaba meditation can be seamlessly integrated into daily mindfulness practices. It aids in reducing stress, enhancing focus, and promoting a balanced emotional state. The practice is not just about the activation of an energy field; it's about cultivating a deeper connection with oneself and the universe.

Common Misconceptions and Challenges

Merkaba meditation, while profound, is often shrouded in misconceptions. It is not exclusive to ascended masters; anyone can practice and benefit from it. Beginners may find the concept complex, but with patience, practice, and possibly guidance from experienced practitioners, its transformative potential can be unlocked.

Merkaba meditation, through its unique blend of sacred geometry, breathwork, and visualization, offers a pathway to spiritual awakening, self-discovery, and mindfulness. It stands as a powerful tool in the journey towards self-actualization and higher consciousness.

MERKABA FOR HEALING AND EMOTIONAL WELL-BEING

The Essence of Merkaba in Healing

The Merkaba, an ancient symbol representing the integration of body, spirit, and light, is believed to possess potent healing properties. These properties are not limited to the physical realm but extend to emotional and spiritual dimensions, providing a holistic approach to well-being.

Balancing and Aligning the Chakras

Central to Merkaba's healing potential is its ability to balance and align the chakras, the energy centers within the body. By focusing on the Merkaba, practitioners can harmonize these centers, enhancing their overall vitality and promoting physical, emotional, and spiritual balance.

Enhancing Energetic Protection

The Merkaba serves as a shield, protecting against negative energies and external influences. This energetic barrier is crucial in maintaining a sense of balance and well-being, allowing individuals to navigate life with greater clarity and positivity.

Emotional Healing and Clearing Negative Energy

Merkaba meditation aids in releasing stagnant emotions, contributing to emotional well-being and inner peace. This process involves cleansing the aura or energy field, thereby facilitating emotional balance and clarity.

Facilitating Spiritual Growth and Transformation

Engaging with the Merkaba symbol activates dormant energies, opening doors to higher consciousness and expanded awareness. It serves as a tool for spiritual growth, enabling connections with higher realms and divine guidance.

Incorporating Crystals for Amplified Healing

Integrating crystals such as amethyst and clear quartz with Merkaba practices enhances their healing effects. These crystals, known for their unique energetic properties, can amplify meditation sessions or be worn as jewelry, providing continuous support.

Connection with Source Energy

The Merkaba is closely linked to source energy, enabling practitioners to align with their soul intentions and manifest desired realities. This connection fosters spiritual alignment and a sense of unity with the universe.

Raising Vibrations

Working with the Merkaba can elevate one's vibrational

frequency, stimulating the flow of positive energy. This elevation leads to feelings of joy, rejuvenation, and a deeper connection with one's true desires.

Cleansing Chakras and Releasing Blockages

The protective powers of the Merkaba extend to clearing chakra blockages, essential for the free flow of energy. Releasing these blockages enhances overall well-being and aligns individuals with their full potential.

Merkaba Meditation Techniques

Merkaba meditation involves a series of breaths and visualizations designed to activate the energy field. This practice expands awareness, cleanses chakras, nurtures intuition, and fosters a deep connection with the self.

Overcoming Challenges in Merkaba Meditation

While beneficial, Merkaba meditation can be complex and challenging. It is essential to approach it with patience and, if necessary, seek guidance from experienced practitioners. Regular practice and perseverance can unlock its transformative potential.

Merkaba, as a tool for healing and emotional well-being, offers a path to holistic health and spiritual growth. Its benefits range from chakra balancing to emotional cleansing and spiritual transformation, making it a profound resource for those seeking inner harmony and growth.

MERKABA IN EVERYDAY LIFE

Embracing Merkaba in Daily Practices

Integrating Merkaba principles into daily life for spiritual growth involves understanding and embracing its sacred geometry and transformative power. The Merkaba, represented by two interlocking tetrahedrons, is a symbol of balance, harmony, and unity between various aspects of existence. It facilitates energy flow and aids in connecting with higher consciousness.

Meditation and Mindfulness

Daily meditation with the Merkaba symbol enhances spiritual practices. Focusing on the Merkaba during meditation aligns energies, promotes deep relaxation, and inner peace. The visualization of the Merkaba serves as a focal point, aiding concentration and heightening awareness.

Chakra Balancing

The Merkaba symbol aids in chakra balancing. Each point of the star corresponds to one of the seven main chakras. Visualizing or physically placing the Merkaba near these energy centers restores balance and harmony to the chakras.

Astral Travel and Accessing Higher Realms

In deeper states of meditation, the Merkaba is a tool for astral travel, transcending physical limitations, and exploring higher realms. Activating the personal energetic field facilitates out-of-body experiences and connects with the spiritual domain.

Daily Integration for Increased Self-Awareness

Incorporating the Merkaba into daily routines enhances self-awareness. Working with this sacred geometry makes one more attuned to thoughts, emotions, and actions, leading to a deeper self-understanding and conscious life choices.

Enhancing Intuition

Regular engagement with the Merkaba sharpens intuitive abilities. The activation of energy centers, especially the third eye chakra, enhances intuition, guiding better decision-making and life navigation.

Energetic Protection

The Merkaba symbol acts as a protective shield against negative energies. It helps maintain energetic boundaries, contributing to a balanced and well-being state in daily life.

Clearing Negative Energy and Emotional Healing

The Merkaba aids in cleansing negative energy from the aura, releasing stagnant emotions, and promoting emotional well-being and inner peace. Its protective nature also fosters mental clarity and positivity.

Facilitating Spiritual Growth and Transformation

Engaging with the Merkaba symbol activates dormant energies, opening doors to higher consciousness, spiritual growth, and divine connection. It serves as a bridge to spiritual realms and guardian angels.

Incorporating Crystals for Enhanced Effect

Using crystals like amethyst and clear quartz alongside the Merkaba amplifies healing and meditative effects. These crystals can be integrated into meditation or worn as jewelry for continuous energetic support.

Understanding Sacred Geometry

Sacred geometry underpins the formation and symbolism of the Merkaba. Understanding these geometrical shapes and patterns reveals the Merkaba's significance in various cultural and spiritual contexts.

Application in Daily Life

Incorporating Merkaba principles into everyday life enhances spiritual practices, promotes well-being, and facilitates personal growth. Whether it's through meditation, chakra balancing, or energy protection, the Merkaba symbol offers a holistic approach to spiritual enlightenment and self-discovery.

MERKABA ACROSS CULTURES

MERKABA IN DIFFERENT SPIRITUAL TRADITIONS

Hinduism and Merkaba

In Hinduism, Merkaba finds parallels in the concept of the "Sri Yantra," a sacred geometrical symbol representing the cosmos. The Sri Yantra consists of nine interlocking triangles surrounded by two circles of lotus petals, embodying the union of the masculine and feminine divine. This symbol aligns closely with Merkaba's integration of opposing energies, reflecting a balance of spiritual forces.

Buddhism and the Merkaba

Buddhism, particularly in its Vajrayana tradition, embraces sacred geometry in the form of mandalas. These intricate, geometric designs are meditation aids, symbolizing the universe's impermanence. The Kalachakra mandala, with its detailed geometrical layers, shares similarities with the Merkaba, serving as a tool for enlightenment and a representation of higher consciousness.

Christian Mysticism and Merkaba

Christian mysticism, although not explicitly referencing Merkaba, has elements akin to it. The concept of "Light Body," often depicted

in religious art as a halo or aura surrounding holy figures, bears resemblance to Merkaba's light vehicle. This representation aligns with Merkaba's role as a vehicle for spiritual ascension and connection with the divine.

Sufism and Merkaba

In Sufism, the mystical branch of Islam, the concept of "soul ascension" and journeying towards divine love mirrors the Merkaba's purpose. Sufi practices like whirling (as seen in the Mevlevi Order) symbolize the soul's journey, reflecting Merkaba's theme of spiritual movement and transformation.

Taoism and Merkaba

Taoism emphasizes balance and harmony, concepts central to the Merkaba. The Taijitu or Yin-Yang symbol, representing interconnected, opposing forces in balance, echoes Merkaba's theme of harmonizing dual energies. The Merkaba's structure and purpose resonate with Taoist principles of flow and equilibrium in the spiritual journey.

Indigenous Traditions and Merkaba

Many indigenous cultures have concepts akin to Merkaba, often seen in their art and spiritual practices. The emphasis on nature, spirit, and cosmos in indigenous beliefs parallels Merkaba's focus on unity and cosmic connection. These traditions often use symbolic geometrical shapes in their rituals, aligning with Merkaba's sacred geometry.

Contemporary Spirituality and Merkaba

In modern spiritual movements, Merkaba has been adopted as a symbol of metaphysical balance and a tool for meditation. It's seen as a means to access higher consciousness and align with universal energies. This integration into various spiritual practices highlights Merkaba's universal appeal and adaptability across cultures and beliefs.

Merkaba, transcending its origins in Jewish mysticism, has found resonance in various spiritual traditions worldwide. Each culture integrates it uniquely, yet the core themes of balance, spiritual journey, and cosmic connection remain consistent. This universality underscores Merkaba's significance as a timeless and borderless symbol in the quest for spiritual understanding and enlightenment.

COMPARATIVE STUDY OF SACRED GEOMETRICAL SYMBOLS

Merkaba and the Flower of Life

The Flower of Life, a symbol found in various ancient cultures, is a geometric pattern consisting of multiple evenly-spaced, overlapping circles. This symbol is foundational in sacred geometry, as it is believed to represent the basic patterns of life itself. The Merkaba is directly related to this symbol, as it is formed from the Flower of Life's pattern. The Merkaba, a star tetrahedron, is seen as a 3-dimensional aspect of this 2-dimensional symbol, indicating a progression from the earthly plane to the transcendent.

Sri Yantra and Merkaba

The Sri Yantra, prominent in Hindu Tantra, is composed of nine interlocking triangles that radiate out from the central point. It represents the cosmos and the human body. The Merkaba, similar in its representation of the cosmos and the human spiritual journey, shares with the Sri Yantra the principle of interconnectedness of the individual with the universe. Both symbols emphasize the journey from the material to the spiritual.

The Celtic Knot and Merkaba

The Celtic Knot, a symbol with no beginning or end, is prevalent in Celtic culture and represents the interconnectedness and continuity of life. While the Merkaba also signifies infinite energy, its emphasis on duality and balance — the interplay of the male and female energies — provides a complementary perspective to the Celtic Knot's theme of eternity and unity.

The Yin-Yang and Merkaba

The Yin-Yang symbol from Chinese Taoism represents dual forces in harmonious balance. This concept of duality and balance is at the core of the Merkaba as well, which balances the opposing energies of Earth and Cosmos, male and female. Both symbols emphasize the necessity of balance in achieving higher states of being.

Mandala and Merkaba

Mandalas, used in various spiritual traditions, are intricate geometric patterns that represent the universe. They are tools for meditation and spiritual guidance. The Merkaba, similarly, is used in meditation practices to align spiritual, mental, and physical planes. Both serve as spiritual maps, guiding the individual in their journey towards enlightenment.

The Caduceus and Merkaba

The Caduceus, an ancient Greek symbol of two snakes winding

around a winged staff, is often associated with balance, healing, and transformation. The Merkaba, with its interlocking triangles, symbolizes the integration of spirit and matter, similar to the Caduceus's representation of the unification of opposites, contributing to a holistic understanding of transformation and ascension.

The Ankh and Merkaba

The Ankh, an ancient Egyptian symbol resembling a cross with a loop at the top, represents life and eternal life. The Merkaba, often associated with the journey of the soul and spiritual rebirth, complements the Ankh's emphasis on life and immortality. Both embody the concept of life beyond the physical realm.

The comparative study of sacred geometrical symbols like the Flower of Life, Sri Yantra, Celtic Knot, Yin-Yang, Mandala, Caduceus, and Ankh with the Merkaba highlights a universal theme in spiritual traditions: the interconnectedness of life, the importance of balance and harmony, and the journey from the physical to the spiritual. Each symbol, while unique in its cultural and historical context, shares with the Merkaba the profound message of spiritual unity and transformation.

MERKABA'S INFLUENCE ON ART AND ARCHITECTURE

Historical Context

Merkaba, derived from ancient Hebrew, symbolizes a 'chariot' and has been a cornerstone of visionary contemplation among Jewish mystics since at least the 1st century AD. This mystical form, characterized by two interlocked tetrahedrons forming a three-dimensional Star of David, emerged as a significant emblem in Merkabah mysticism. It flourished during 200-700 CE, playing a crucial role in the literature of Chassidei Ashkenaz during the Middle Ages.

Merkaba in Artistic Representations

The Merkaba symbol, embodying light ('mer'), spirit ('ka'), and body ('ba'), has deeply influenced artistic expressions. Its depiction in sacred geometry has been an integral part of various art forms. This symbol represents not only a fusion of divine energies but also serves as a powerful visual metaphor in art. The intertwining of feminine and masculine energies within its structure offers a rich canvas for artists to explore themes of spiritual balance and unity.

Fashion and Merkaba

In contemporary times, the Merkaba has transcended traditional spiritual contexts, notably influencing the fashion industry. For instance, the fashion collective threeASFOUR's MER KA BA project, presented at The Jewish Museum in New York, integrated the Merkaba into avant-garde couture. This collection, inspired by sacred geometry and tile patterns from synagogues, churches, and mosques, showcased how ancient symbols like the Merkaba could be reinterpreted in modern design aesthetics.

Merkaba and Architecture

The architectural realm has also seen the incorporation of Merkaba-inspired designs. The concept of sacred geometry, to which Merkaba is central, has influenced the creation of sacred spaces and structures. The balance and harmony inherent in the Merkaba's geometry have guided architects in designing buildings that resonate with spiritual symbolism. This influence extends from ancient structures to contemporary architectural marvels, where the principles of sacred geometry continue to inspire form and function.

Merkaba's Modern Interpretations

In modern art and architecture, Merkaba's influence is evident in the use of its geometric principles. Artists and architects have utilized its form to represent the intertwining of the earthly and the divine, the material and the spiritual. The Merkaba's representation as a vehicle of light and ascension is metaphorically reflected in artworks and architectural designs that strive to transcend the ordinary and reach towards the sublime.

Reflection in Public Spaces

Public art installations and architectural landmarks often incorporate Merkaba-inspired elements to evoke a sense of spiritual transcendence. These installations serve not only as visual spectacles but also as mediums for public engagement with spiritual concepts, often sparking curiosity and contemplation among viewers.

The influence of the Merkaba in art and architecture underscores the timeless appeal of this symbol. From ancient mysticism to modern creative expressions, the Merkaba continues to inspire a wide range of artistic and architectural innovations. It serves as a bridge between the past and the present, between spiritual symbolism and contemporary creativity, thus enriching the cultural and artistic landscape.

THE SCIENCE OF
MERKABA

QUANTUM PHYSICS AND SACRED GEOMETRY

Merkaba and Quantum Physics

Merkaba, a term originating from ancient Hebrew, translates to 'light,' 'spirit,' and 'body.' In the realm of quantum physics, the Merkaba is perceived as a divine light vehicle, signifying the human body's energy field. This field comprises two counter-rotating triangles, symbolizing masculine and feminine energies, and spins at the speed of light. Quantum physics acknowledges the Merkaba as a multi-dimensional being, encompassing the potential for inter-dimensional movement and spiritual ascension. The Merkaba's integration into quantum physics represents a leap in understanding consciousness, as it blends spirituality with the science of energy fields and vibration.

Merkaba in Sacred Geometry

Sacred geometry, a philosophical approach that attributes spiritual significance to geometric shapes, has profound connections with the Merkaba. The Merkaba, represented by two interlocking tetrahedrons, forms a three-dimensional Star of David. Sacred geometry posits that these shapes and patterns underlie the fundamental aspects of life and the universe. The Merkaba, as an integral part of sacred geometry, embodies the unity and balance between masculine (action, strength) and feminine (receptivity, nurturing) energies. It serves as a reminder of the importance of harmony in spiritual transformation and the interconnectedness of body, mind, and spirit.

Merkaba's Healing Properties

The Merkaba is believed to possess powerful healing properties, influencing physical, emotional, and spiritual well-being. Its geometrical shape is used in meditation and energy healing practices for aligning and balancing chakras. This alignment fosters a sense of balance, vitality, and emotional well-being. Additionally, the Merkaba acts as a protective shield against negative energies, maintaining energetic boundaries and contributing to a balanced state of being.

Astral Travel and Higher Consciousness

In deeper meditative states, practitioners use the Merkaba for astral travel or out-of-body experiences. It is viewed as a gateway to higher consciousness, allowing access to wisdom and guidance from higher dimensions. The Merkaba symbolizes the potential for spiritual growth and transformation, activating dormant energies within and connecting to higher realms of existence.

Merkaba and Planetary Grid

Recent studies have suggested that Earth's planetary grid could be an icosahedron, a form found within Metatron's cube, a sacred geometric form that includes the Merkaba. This grid connects high magnetic field locations like the Bermuda Triangle, sacred monuments, and other energetically significant sites. The

Merkaba, as part of this sacred geometry, implies a deeper connection between individual consciousness and the Earth's energetic grid, suggesting a collective journey towards unity and harmony.

The Transcendental Nature of Merkaba

The Merkaba, within the scope of sacred geometry, is seen as a transcendental form. It is capable of infinite expansion and contraction while maintaining its shape, symbolizing the boundless nature of consciousness. This transcendental quality reflects the Merkaba's role in spiritual practices, where it is used to transcend physical limitations and explore higher dimensions of consciousness.

The convergence of quantum physics and sacred geometry in understanding the Merkaba marks a significant shift in our approach to spirituality and consciousness. The Merkaba stands at the intersection of these two fields, embodying principles of balance, unity, and transformation, and offering a path to higher states of being and deeper understanding of the universe.

Merkaba and Quantum Entanglement

The concept of Merkaba aligns with the quantum physics principle of entanglement, where two particles remain connected regardless of distance, reflecting an intrinsic unity. The Merkaba symbolizes this interconnectedness at a cosmic level, suggesting that our individual consciousness is entangled with the universal consciousness. This connection enables a deeper understanding of our place in the cosmos and the potential to access higher dimensions of reality.

Quantum Field Theory and Merkaba

In Quantum Field Theory (QFT), fields are the fundamental entities, and particles are excitations of these fields. The Merkaba, viewed through the lens of QFT, represents a complex field comprising spiritual and physical aspects of existence. This perspective bridges spiritual experiences and scientific understanding, illustrating how consciousness and matter are deeply intertwined.

Merkaba and the Holographic Universe Theory

The Holographic Universe Theory, which posits that our reality is a projection of higher-dimensional processes, resonates with the Merkaba's representation of multi-dimensional travel. The Merkaba, as a vehicle for spiritual ascension, supports this theory by suggesting that our three-dimensional experience is just one aspect of a much larger, interconnected reality.

The Merkaba and Vibrational Frequencies

Quantum physics recognizes that everything in the universe vibrates at specific frequencies, and the Merkaba is no exception. By aligning with the vibrational frequencies of the Merkaba, individuals can elevate their consciousness and potentially influence their physical reality, resonating with the quantum concept of reality being shaped by observation and intention.

Consciousness and Quantum Mechanics

The role of consciousness in quantum mechanics – particularly in the collapse of the wave function – parallels the Merkaba's function in spiritual practices. The Merkaba symbolizes the power of consciousness to transcend physical boundaries and access higher states of awareness, mirroring quantum theories that suggest consciousness plays a fundamental role in shaping reality.

Merkaba in Neuroscientific Research

Neuroscientific research into meditation and consciousness is beginning to uncover connections with ancient practices involving the Merkaba. Brain imaging studies of meditation show changes in brain activity that correlate with states of higher consciousness, supporting the idea that the Merkaba meditation can facilitate profound mental and spiritual experiences.

The integration of Merkaba in the realm of quantum physics and sacred geometry represents a harmonious blend of science and spirituality. This synthesis offers a more comprehensive understanding of the universe and our place within it, highlighting the Merkaba as a key to unlocking the mysteries of consciousness and reality.

MERKABA AND CONSCIOUSNESS STUDIES

The Intersection of Consciousness and Merkaba

Consciousness studies, an interdisciplinary field spanning psychology, neuroscience, and philosophy, have begun to explore connections with the concept of Merkaba. Let's look at how the Merkaba, a symbol of spiritual ascension and energy fields, relates to human consciousness and its various dimensions and structures.

Consciousness Theories and the Merkaba

Several theories in consciousness studies propose different understandings of how the brain produces conscious experience. The Merkaba's concept aligns with these theories as a representation of the energy field surrounding the human body, suggesting a complex relationship between consciousness and spiritual energy fields. This relationship highlights the potential multi-dimensional nature of consciousness, resonating with the Merkaba's embodiment of higher spiritual realms.

Epistemological and Ontological Questions

Consciousness research raises several key questions, such as the content, structure, and dimensions of consciousness. These questions also apply to the study of the Merkaba, as it is believed to be a vehicle for spiritual consciousness. The exploration of how consciousness is located in the world, its relation to the physical realm, and how it is distributed aligns with the Merkaba's representation of the interconnection between the physical and spiritual worlds.

Merkaba and Cognitive Processes

Merkaba is increasingly being studied in relation to cognitive processes, such as how consciousness enables various cognitive capacities, including intuition and self-awareness. The Merkaba's role in meditation and energy healing practices is seen as a way to enhance these cognitive capacities, suggesting a deeper connection between the symbol and cognitive aspects of consciousness.

Consciousness Research: Methodologies and Challenges

Contemporary consciousness research utilizes a variety of methodologies, including introspection, observation, and reasoning approaches. These methods offer insights into the phenomenological features of consciousness, paralleling the practices used in Merkaba meditations and visualizations. The challenges in consciousness research, such as interpreting subjective experiences and understanding complex cognitive phenomena, are similarly encountered in studies and practices involving the Merkaba.

Merkaba in Neuroscientific Studies

Neuroscience, a key player in consciousness research, investigates the neural correlates of consciousness. Studies on meditation, including those involving the Merkaba, reveal significant neural changes, suggesting a scientific basis for the spiritual experiences associated with the Merkaba. This area of research bridges the gap between spiritual practices and scientific understanding.

Quantum Consciousness and Merkaba

Quantum consciousness studies, exploring the role of quantum mechanics in consciousness, intersect with the Merkaba concept. The Merkaba, as a symbol of energy fields and spiritual transformation, could potentially be explained through quantum theories of consciousness. This link provides a more comprehensive understanding of consciousness that encompasses both physical and spiritual dimensions.

Merkaba and Global Consciousness

Global consciousness studies, investigating the interconnectedness of human consciousness, resonate with the Merkaba's symbolism of unity and spiritual connection. The concept of Merkaba, representing a collective journey towards higher consciousness, aligns with research suggesting a unified field of consciousness that transcends individual experiences.

The integration of Merkaba in consciousness studies represents a significant step towards understanding the complex relationship between spirituality and consciousness. By exploring this ancient symbol within the framework of modern scientific research, we gain deeper insights into the nature of consciousness and its connection to higher spiritual realms.

Merkaba and Altered States of Consciousness

Research into altered states of consciousness, such as those achieved through meditation or psychedelic experiences, often intersects with the concept of the Merkaba. These states are believed to facilitate access to higher realms of consciousness, a key aspect of the Merkaba. This convergence offers insights into how spiritual practices involving the Merkaba might alter perception and cognition.

Merkaba in Consciousness Expansion

The role of the Merkaba in consciousness expansion is a focal point in many studies. It is posited that engaging with the Merkaba, through meditation or visualization, can lead to expanded awareness and a deeper connection with the universe. This aligns with the idea that consciousness is not just a product of the brain but a fundamental aspect of the universe, interconnected with all forms of existence.

The Merkaba and Consciousness Evolution

The evolution of consciousness, a concept that suggests a progressive development of awareness and understanding, can be linked to the Merkaba. As a symbol of spiritual ascension, the Merkaba is seen as a tool for facilitating this evolutionary process, helping individuals tap into higher levels of consciousness and understanding.

Merkaba, Mindfulness, and Mental Health

The integration of Merkaba principles in mindfulness and mental health practices highlights its potential in enhancing psychological well-being. By focusing on the balance and unity represented by the Merkaba, individuals can achieve a state of mental harmony, beneficial for coping with stress and emotional challenges.

Neuroplasticity and the Merkaba

Recent studies in neuroplasticity – the brain's ability to reorganize itself – have shown that practices involving the Merkaba can lead to significant changes in brain structure and function. These changes are associated with improved cognitive abilities, emotional regulation, and enhanced consciousness levels.

Collective Consciousness and the Merkaba

The concept of collective consciousness, which posits a shared pool of knowledge and understanding among humans, resonates with the Merkaba's symbolism of unity. The Merkaba's role in connecting individuals to higher planes of existence suggests that it might also facilitate a deeper connection to this collective consciousness.

Future Directions in Merkaba and Consciousness Research

As the field of consciousness studies continues to evolve, future research will likely delve deeper into the Merkaba's role in understanding consciousness. This includes exploring its potential in therapeutic settings, its influence on cognitive and emotional processes, and its broader implications for understanding the human experience.

Merkaba's incorporation into consciousness studies marks a significant step towards bridging the gap between science and spirituality. By exploring this ancient symbol through the lens of modern consciousness research, we are opening new doors to understanding the intricate relationship between the mind, the spirit, and the universe.

NEUROSCIENCE AND MEDITATION

Brain Activity Modulation through Meditation

Neuroscientific research has revealed that meditation practices, including those associated with the Merkaba, can modulate brain activity. Different forms of meditation, such as mindfulness, Vipassana, and Transcendental Meditation (TM), have been shown to activate various regions of the brain, including the dorsolateral and medial prefrontal cortexes. These areas are associated with executive attention, mood, and immune function, and their activation indicates the profound impact of meditation on cognitive and emotional processes.

Structural Changes in the Brain

Studies have documented structural alterations in the brain as a result of long-term meditation practice. These changes include increased grey matter density in the brain stem and other regions related to attention, memory, and emotional regulation. Such findings suggest that meditation can lead to enduring changes in the brain, enhancing its functioning and potentially leading to improved mental health outcomes.

Meditation's Impact on Emotional Regulation

Meditation has been found to significantly influence emotional regulation, with particular activation and deactivation in key brain regions. Practices involving the Merkaba are likely to engage

similar neural mechanisms, facilitating a balanced emotional state and improved stress management. This aligns with the Merkaba's role in promoting harmony and balance, both spiritually and neurologically.

Neuroplasticity and Enhanced Cognitive Functions

The concept of neuroplasticity, the brain's ability to reorganize itself, is central to understanding the effects of meditation on the brain. Merkaba meditation, like other forms, can lead to neuroplastic changes, enhancing cognitive functions such as memory, attention, and self-regulation. These changes demonstrate the brain's remarkable adaptability and the potential of meditation to foster cognitive and emotional growth.

Meditation, Mindfulness, and Stress Reduction

Meditation practices, particularly mindfulness-based stress reduction (MBSR), have been validated in scientific studies for their efficacy in reducing stress and improving overall well-being. As Merkaba meditation also focuses on mindfulness and balance, it could offer similar benefits, potentially serving as an effective tool for managing stress and enhancing mental health.

Meditation and Autonomic Nervous System Regulation

Research indicates that meditation can alter the interaction between the central and autonomic nervous systems. This interaction is crucial for maintaining physiological balance and is reflected in improved stress response, heart rate variability, and overall physical health. Merkaba meditation's focus on energy fields and balance may contribute to these beneficial effects, harmonizing the body's internal processes.

Future Research Directions

Ongoing neuroscience research continues to explore the extensive effects of meditation on brain function and structure. Future studies may delve deeper into the specific impacts of Merkaba meditation, providing further insights into its unique contributions to cognitive, emotional, and physiological well-being.

The integration of neuroscience and meditation, including the study of the Merkaba, offers profound insights into the human mind and body. These studies not only validate ancient spiritual practices but also open new avenues for enhancing mental health and cognitive abilities.

Enhanced Attention and Mindfulness

Neuroscientific studies have documented that meditation, including practices centered around the Merkaba, enhances attentional capacities and mindfulness. This is reflected in increased activation in regions of the brain associated with executive attention and self-regulation. Such findings suggest that Merkaba meditation can significantly improve cognitive functions related to focus, decision-making, and emotional control.

Merkaba Meditation and Neural Correlates

Investigations into the neural correlates of focused meditation reveal changes in brain regions key to meta-awareness, sensory awareness, and emotional regulation. These alterations in brain function and structure support the idea that Merkaba meditation not only impacts spiritual experiences but also brings about tangible changes in the brain. This evidence provides a scientific basis for the transformative effects attributed to Merkaba practices.

Meditation's Effect on Neural Connectivity

Meditation has been shown to influence neural connectivity, altering the way different brain regions communicate and coordinate with each other. This restructuring of neural networks is crucial for cognitive and emotional processing, and practices involving the Merkaba are likely to contribute to these beneficial changes, promoting mental clarity and emotional stability.

Meditation and Stress Response

Scientific studies have highlighted meditation's impact on reducing stress response, with changes observed in the activation of brain regions associated with stress and anxiety. Merkaba meditation, with its focus on balance and spiritual alignment, may offer similar benefits, helping practitioners manage stress more effectively and maintain emotional equilibrium.

Mind-Body Connection

The research into meditation and neuroscience underscores the deep connection between the mind and body. By influencing brain activity and structure, meditation practices like those involving the Merkaba can lead to improved physical health outcomes, such as lower stress levels, better immune function, and enhanced overall well-being.

The intersection of neuroscience and meditation, particularly in the context of the Merkaba, provides a rich field of study. It offers insights into how ancient spiritual practices can bring about profound changes in the brain, enhancing mental, emotional, and physical health. As research continues, the understanding of how the Merkaba influences the brain and consciousness will likely deepen, further bridging the gap between science and spirituality.

DEEPENING THE
PRACTICE

ADVANCED MERKABA MEDITATION TECHNIQUES

Embarking on advanced Merkaba meditation techniques represents a deeper dive into the mystical practice, offering profound experiences and insights. These techniques require a nuanced understanding of the Merkaba, along with a disciplined approach to meditation.

Detailed Visualization Techniques: Advanced practitioners engage in complex visualizations of the Merkaba. This involves not only picturing the interlocking tetrahedrons around the body but also perceiving the flow of energy within this sacred geometry. The visualization extends to feeling the rotational movement of the Merkaba field, often synchronized with breath work.

Breath Work and Pranic Energies: At this level, practitioners master the art of using their breath to control and channel pranic energies. Breath patterns become more intricate, often involving specific rhythms and depths to stimulate the energy centers (chakras) within the body. This breath work is fundamental in raising one's vibrational frequency to align with higher consciousness.

Activation of the Light Body: A key aspect of advanced Merkaba meditation is the activation of the light body. Practitioners focus on expanding their consciousness beyond the physical realm, tapping into higher dimensions of existence. This process is believed to enhance spiritual awareness and connect the practitioner with their higher self.

Integration of the Heart Chakra: Unlike basic techniques, advanced practices place significant emphasis on the heart chakra. This involves nurturing feelings of unconditional love and compassion during meditation. The heart chakra acts as the anchor for higher frequency energies, facilitating a deeper connection with the universal life force.

Astral Projection and Multidimensional Travel: Advanced Merkaba meditation can be a gateway to astral projection and multidimensional travel. Practitioners use their activated Merkaba field as a vehicle to explore other realms and dimensions, gaining spiritual insights and experiences beyond the physical world.

Energy Balancing and Alignment: Advanced techniques include specific exercises for balancing and aligning energies within the body. This might involve directing energy to different chakras or parts of the body, or even projecting healing energy to others or the planet.

Regular Practice and Discipline: As with any advanced practice, consistency is key. Regular meditation sessions are crucial for maintaining the strength and stability of the Merkaba field. Practitioners often dedicate a specific time and space for their practice to achieve the best results.

Mentorship and Community: Engaging with a mentor or a community of practitioners can be incredibly beneficial. Advanced practices can sometimes lead to intense experiences, and guidance from experienced individuals can provide essential support and insight.

Advanced Merkaba meditation techniques offer a profound journey into spiritual realms, requiring dedication, practice, and a deep understanding of sacred geometry and energy work. These practices unlock higher levels of consciousness and facilitate a stronger connection with the universal energy, aiding in personal and spiritual growth.

MERKABA AND
ASTRAL TRAVEL

Merkaba and astral travel form a profound intersection in spiritual practice, offering an expansive view of consciousness beyond the physical body. Let's delve deeply into the nuances of utilizing Merkaba for astral travel, a journey that transcends ordinary reality.

Fundamentals of Astral Travel: Astral travel, or astral projection, is the act of the conscious mind journeying outside the physical body. It is not limited by physical boundaries and can traverse different dimensions or planes of existence. The astral body is believed to be connected to the physical body by a silver cord, ensuring its return after travel.

Merkaba as the Vehicle for Astral Travel: In the realm of astral projection, Merkaba is perceived as a multi-dimensional vehicle, facilitating safe and purposeful travel. The Merkaba field, when properly activated, encases the practitioner in a protective energy field, enabling them to navigate the astral plane.

Preparation for Astral Projection: Key to astral projection is a state of deep relaxation and a clear, focused mind. This is often achieved through meditation and calming techniques. Preparatory practices include grounding exercises and setting clear intentions for the journey.

Techniques for Achieving Astral Projection: Advanced Merkaba meditation involves specific techniques that align the energy fields and chakras, creating the right vibrational state for astral projection. Practitioners visualize their Merkaba field and focus on the intention to travel, allowing the astral body to gently separate from the physical form.

Navigating the Astral Plane: Once in the astral realm, practitioners use their thoughts and intentions to move and explore. It's a realm where thought becomes action instantaneously. Beginners are advised to start with familiar environments before venturing into unknown territories.

Experiences in the Astral Plane: The astral plane is rich with experiences. It's not bound by earthly physics, allowing for incredible encounters and learnings. Practitioners often report meeting spiritual guides, accessing ancient wisdom, and gaining profound insights.

Safety and Ethical Practices: Safety in astral travel is paramount. The Merkaba field serves as a guardian, and it's important to return to the physical body at the first sign of discomfort or disorientation. Ethical practices involve respecting the spaces and entities encountered and not using astral travel for harmful or invasive purposes.

Integration of Astral Experiences: Post-astral travel, practitioners often journal or meditate to process and integrate their experiences. This can lead to a deeper understanding of oneself and the nature of reality.

Merkaba, when used in conjunction with astral travel, opens up new dimensions of spiritual exploration and understanding. It offers a unique pathway to access higher knowledge and to experience the vastness of consciousness beyond the physical domain.

THE MERKABA AND KUNDALINI ENERGY

The intricate relationship between the Merkaba and Kundalini energy is a key aspect of spiritual development. Let's explore how the Merkaba field interacts with and supports the awakening of Kundalini energy, leading to profound transformative experiences.

Understanding Kundalini Energy: Kundalini energy is often described as a dormant, coiled force at the base of the spine. When awakened, this energy travels up through the chakras to the crown, leading to spiritual enlightenment. This process is marked by profound physical, emotional, and spiritual changes.

Merkaba as a Support for Kundalini Awakening: The Merkaba field plays a vital role in supporting and stabilizing the Kundalini energy as it ascends. The geometric energy field of the Merkaba helps in maintaining balance and providing a protective energy environment.

Preparation for Kundalini Awakening: Before attempting to awaken Kundalini energy, it is essential to have a strong foundation in Merkaba meditation. This ensures that the energy system is balanced and ready to handle the powerful surge of Kundalini.

Balancing Chakras with Merkaba: The practice involves using the Merkaba field to balance and harmonize the chakras, creating a smooth path for the ascent of Kundalini. Each chakra is visualized and energized within the Merkaba field, aligning the energy centers.

Techniques for Raising Kundalini: Specific breathing techniques and meditations are used in conjunction with the Merkaba field to gently awaken and guide the Kundalini energy. This process should be approached with respect and caution, as Kundalini is a powerful force.

Experiencing the Kundalini Rise: The rising of Kundalini through the chakras can bring about intense experiences, including visions, emotional release, and a profound sense of connection with the universe. The Merkaba field aids in integrating these experiences, ensuring a harmonious journey.

Handling Intense Energy Surges: At times, the awakening of Kundalini can lead to overwhelming energy surges. Here, the Merkaba field serves as a stabilizing force, helping to distribute and manage these energies safely throughout the body.

Integration and Transformation: The ultimate goal of combining Merkaba with Kundalini practices is to achieve a state of spiritual awakening and transformation. This journey transforms the practitioner's perception of self and the universe, leading to a life that is more aligned with spiritual principles.

The conjunction of Merkaba and Kundalini practices offers a profound path toward spiritual awakening and personal transformation. This journey requires dedication, understanding, and respect for the powerful energies at play.

PERSONAL
TRANSFORMATION

MERKABA FOR SELF-DISCOVERY AND AWARENESS

The practice of Merkaba for self-discovery and awareness is an enriching journey into the depths of one's being. Let's explore how the Merkaba enhances introspection and self-awareness, fostering a deeper understanding of the self and one's place in the universe.

Merkaba as a Tool for Introspection: Merkaba meditation is not just a practice for spiritual ascension but also a profound method for self-reflection. By focusing inward while encompassed in the Merkaba field, practitioners can delve into their subconscious, uncovering hidden thoughts, emotions, and patterns.

Enhancing Mindfulness and Presence: Merkaba practices cultivate a heightened state of mindfulness and presence. This enhanced awareness extends beyond meditation sessions, permeating daily life, and activities. Practitioners learn to live in the moment, fully engaging with their experiences.

Emotional Awareness and Management: Through Merkaba, individuals gain greater insight into their emotional landscape. This awareness allows for better management of emotions, leading to a more balanced and harmonious life. Techniques include observing emotions without judgment and using the

Merkaba field to transform negative emotional energy.

Developing Self-Awareness: Merkaba meditation encourages a deeper understanding of personal values, beliefs, and motives. This self-awareness is pivotal in personal growth and development, as it leads to more conscious decision-making and aligns actions with one's true self.

Overcoming Mental Barriers: The practice is also instrumental in identifying and overcoming mental and emotional blocks. By bringing these to the surface within the safe space of the Merkaba field, individuals can work through and release these barriers, paving the way for personal growth and freedom.

Cultivating Inner Peace and Balance: Regular Merkaba meditation nurtures a sense of inner peace and balance. This tranquility is not just limited to the meditative state but becomes a constant presence, aiding in facing life's challenges with equanimity.

Expanding Intuition and Inner Wisdom: As practitioners deepen their Merkaba practice, they often find their intuition and inner wisdom expanding. This inner guidance becomes a reliable source for making life decisions and understanding one's path in life.

Practical Application in Daily Life: The insights and learnings from Merkaba meditation are not just theoretical but are highly applicable in everyday life. From improving relationships to enhancing career choices, the practice offers practical benefits that stem from a deeper understanding of the self.

The use of Merkaba in the journey of self-discovery and awareness opens up a world of introspection and personal insight. It is a path that leads to a deeper understanding of oneself and a more conscious, fulfilled life.

OVERCOMING CHALLENGES WITH MERKABA

Merkaba's principles provide a unique perspective and tools for overcoming life's challenges. Let's examine how Merkaba can be applied to navigate through various difficulties, aiding in personal transformation and resilience.

Understanding Challenges Through Merkaba: Merkaba teaches viewing challenges not as obstacles but as opportunities for growth and learning. The Merkaba field, symbolizing infinite possibilities, encourages a mindset shift, allowing individuals to approach problems with a sense of creativity and openness.

Emotional Resilience with Merkaba: The practice of Merkaba meditation can significantly aid in building emotional resilience. By creating a balanced and harmonized energy field, practitioners are better equipped to handle emotional stress and upheaval. Techniques focus on maintaining a centered state amidst life's turbulence.

Merkaba in Relationship Dynamics: Challenges in personal relationships can be navigated through the principles of Merkaba. By fostering qualities such as empathy, understanding, and non-judgment, Merkaba practices can improve communication and foster deeper connections with others.

Facing Fear and Doubt: Merkaba helps confront and transcend fears and doubts. By aligning with the protective and empowering energy of the Merkaba field, individuals can find the courage to face their fears and transform doubt into a force for positive action and confidence.

Physical Well-being and Merkaba: Beyond the spiritual and emotional realms, Merkaba practices can also contribute to physical well-being. The energy work involved in Merkaba meditation can enhance the body's natural healing processes and aid in overcoming physical challenges.

Merkaba in Achieving Personal Goals: Applying Merkaba principles can be incredibly effective in setting and achieving personal and professional goals. The focus on intention and energy alignment helps manifest desired outcomes, while the Merkaba field provides a supportive environment for growth and success.

Spiritual Growth Amidst Adversity: Challenges often serve as catalysts for deep spiritual growth. Merkaba practices enable individuals to find spiritual lessons in their struggles, turning every challenge into an opportunity for profound personal development.

Community Support in Merkaba Practice: Engaging with a community of Merkaba practitioners can provide valuable support and shared wisdom in overcoming life's challenges. The collective energy and shared experiences of a group can amplify the benefits of Merkaba practices.

The Merkaba offers powerful tools for overcoming a wide array of life's challenges. By harnessing its principles and practices, individuals can transform their struggles into stepping stones for personal growth, resilience, and transformation.

MERKABA AND PERSONAL GROWTH

Merkaba's role in personal growth is profound and multifaceted. Let's delve into how engaging with Merkaba practices fosters personal transformation, facilitating a journey towards a more aware, empowered, and fulfilled self.

Merkaba as a Catalyst for Personal Evolution: Merkaba is not just a tool for spiritual awakening; it's a catalyst for overall personal growth. By aligning the physical, mental, emotional, and spiritual aspects, Merkaba sets the stage for holistic development.

Self-Discovery through Merkaba: The practice encourages deep introspection, leading to self-discovery. Understanding one's true nature, desires, and life purpose becomes clearer as one delves deeper into Merkaba meditation.

Empowerment and Confidence: Regular engagement with Merkaba builds inner strength and confidence. As practitioners become more attuned to their Merkaba field, they often report feeling more empowered to make decisions and take actions aligned with their true selves.

Merkaba and Emotional Intelligence: Emotional intelligence is enhanced through Merkaba practices. Practitioners learn to better understand, manage, and express their emotions, leading to improved relationships and social interactions.

Overcoming Limiting Beliefs: Merkaba meditation helps in identifying and releasing limiting beliefs that hinder personal growth. Through visualization and energy work, these negative thought patterns are transformed, opening up new possibilities for personal achievement.

Enhancing Creativity and Problem-Solving: By tapping into higher states of consciousness, Merkaba practitioners often experience increased creativity and improved problem-solving abilities. This is attributed to accessing broader perspectives and deeper wisdom.

Integrating Spiritual Insights into Daily Life: One of the key aspects of personal growth with Merkaba is the integration of spiritual insights into everyday life. This integration leads to living a more conscious, purposeful, and fulfilling life.

Merkaba for Lifelong Learning: Personal growth is a continuous journey, and Merkaba supports this by fostering a mindset of lifelong learning and curiosity. Practitioners are encouraged to explore, experiment, and evolve continually.

Merkaba is a powerful tool for personal growth, offering pathways to self-discovery, emotional mastery, and the integration of spiritual wisdom into daily life. It empowers individuals to live their fullest potential, continuously evolve, and contribute positively to their surroundings.

MERKABA IN
MODERN TIMES

MERKABA IN CONTEMPORARY SPIRITUALITY

In the ever-evolving landscape of contemporary spirituality, the ancient concept of Merkaba has found a unique and significant place. Originally rooted in esoteric traditions, Merkaba, symbolizing a light chariot or vehicle, has transcended its traditional boundaries, emerging as a versatile tool in modern spiritual practices.

Merkaba's Resurgence in New Age Movements

At the heart of Merkaba's revival in contemporary spirituality lies its adoption by New Age movements. Here, Merkaba is often interpreted beyond its historical and cultural origins, embodying a universal symbol for spiritual ascension and enlightenment. New Age practitioners view Merkaba as a metaphysical structure, an interdimensional vehicle facilitating a deeper connection with higher realms of consciousness. This interpretation hinges on the belief that Merkaba, when activated through meditation and visualization, enables individuals to traverse spiritual planes, fostering a profound sense of interconnectedness with the universe.

Integration with Holistic Healing Practices

Merkaba's role in modern spirituality extends into the realm of holistic healing. Healers and energy workers incorporate Merkaba into their practices, recognizing its potential in balancing and harmonizing the body's energy field. In this context, Merkaba is often visualized as a rotating field of light, capable of cleansing and rejuvenating the spiritual, emotional, and physical aspects of an individual. This practice is  believed to enhance one's overall well-being, creating a state of equilibrium that supports healing processes.

Merkaba and Meditation Techniques

A significant aspect of Merkaba's contemporary application is its integration into meditation techniques. Practitioners often use Merkaba meditation as a pathway to achieving higher states of consciousness. This meditative practice typically involves visualizing the Merkaba structure surrounding the body, rotating in specific patterns. This visualization is believed to activate the energy fields around the practitioner, facilitating a deep, transformative experience. Through such practices, individuals report experiences of profound inner peace, heightened intuition, and increased self-awareness.

Influence on Personal Development and Self-Awareness

Merkaba has also been embraced as a tool for personal development and self-awareness in modern spirituality. Its geometrical representation as a star tetrahedron is seen as a metaphor for the balance between the physical and spiritual, the earth and cosmos, and the masculine and feminine energies. By meditating on and aligning with the Merkaba, individuals seek to harmonize these dualities within themselves, fostering personal growth and a deeper understanding of their place in the universe.

Adaptation in Art and Cultural Expressions

In the realm of art and cultural expressions, the Merkaba symbol has been adopted widely, often represented in artworks, jewelry, and architectural designs. Artists and designers draw inspiration from its geometric form, infusing their creations with a sense of sacredness and spiritual meaning. This adaptation reflects the growing influence of Merkaba in popular culture, symbolizing a bridge between ancient wisdom and contemporary artistic expression.

Educational and Therapeutic Settings

Beyond its spiritual applications, Merkaba principles have found their way into educational and therapeutic settings. In these environments, the concepts underlying Merkaba are used to facilitate learning, personal development, and emotional healing. Educators and therapists who integrate Merkaba into their methodologies often focus on its aspects of balance, harmony, and interconnectedness, using these principles to foster a supportive and nurturing environment for growth and healing.

Influence on Digital and Virtual Realities

With the advent of digital and virtual realities, Merkaba has also seen an intriguing adaptation. In virtual meditation apps and digital retreats, Merkaba is often presented as a visual and interactive element, enhancing the immersive experience of users. This digital representation allows individuals to explore the Merkaba's geometrical structure in a three-dimensional space, offering a new way to engage with this ancient concept.

The Merkaba, an ancient symbol steeped in mystical traditions, has found a vibrant and diverse role in contemporary spirituality. From its use in holistic healing and meditation to its influence in art and education, Merkaba's journey through modern times showcases its adaptability and enduring relevance. As a bridge between the ancient and the new, Merkaba continues to inspire and facilitate spiritual growth, healing, and self-discovery among seekers of all paths.

Merkaba's Role in Community Building and Collective Practices

In contemporary spirituality, Merkaba's significance extends to the realm of community building and collective practices. Spiritual groups and communities often gather for Merkaba-focused sessions, where participants engage in group meditations, energy work, and discussions centered around the Merkaba's teachings. These gatherings are not just about individual spiritual growth but also about fostering a sense of unity and shared purpose. In these spaces, Merkaba serves as a focal point for collective spiritual experiences, promoting a sense of belonging and mutual support among participants.

Environmental Consciousness and Merkaba

In an age increasingly aware of environmental challenges, Merkaba has been interpreted as a symbol of ecological balance and harmony. This perspective sees the Merkaba as representing the delicate interplay of natural forces, mirroring the balance necessary for a sustainable relationship with our planet. Environmentalists and spiritual practitioners alike use the Merkaba as a tool for meditation and reflection on the interconnectedness of all life, aiming to cultivate a deeper sense of responsibility towards the Earth.

Merkaba in the Digital Age: Online Platforms and Resources

The digital age has further expanded the reach and accessibility of Merkaba teachings. Numerous online platforms, websites, and social media groups are dedicated to sharing knowledge, experiences, and techniques related to Merkaba. These digital resources make the ancient wisdom surrounding Merkaba more accessible to a global audience, enabling a widespread exchange of ideas and practices. Online courses, webinars, and virtual workshops offer guidance on Merkaba meditation and its applications, bridging geographical barriers and creating a worldwide community of practitioners.

The Future Trajectory of Merkaba in Spirituality

Looking ahead, the trajectory of Merkaba in contemporary spirituality seems poised for continued evolution and growth. As individuals and communities become more open to integrating ancient wisdom with modern practices, Merkaba's role is likely to deepen and diversify. Future developments might see an even greater blending of Merkaba principles with scientific understanding, particularly in areas like quantum physics and consciousness studies. This synthesis could offer new insights and applications of Merkaba, further enriching its significance in the spiritual journey of humankind.

MERKABA AND MODERN HEALING PRACTICES

In the realm of modern healing practices, the ancient concept of Merkaba has been revitalized and reimagined, bridging the gap between historical spirituality and contemporary wellness approaches. Recognized for its geometrical perfection and deep spiritual significance, Merkaba offers a unique perspective in the healing arts, resonating with practitioners and individuals seeking holistic well-being.

Merkaba's Integration in Energy Healing

Central to the application of Merkaba in modern healing is its role in energy work. Healers utilize the Merkaba symbol, visualized as a three-dimensional star tetrahedron, to stabilize and rejuvenate the human energy field. This practice is grounded in the belief that the Merkaba structure aligns and balances energy flows within the body, promoting self-healing and connecting individuals to higher dimensions for guidance. In energy healing sessions, practitioners often focus on the Merkaba to facilitate a deeper healing process, tapping into universal energy sources.

Merkaba in Holistic Therapies

Holistic therapists have adopted Merkaba for its perceived ability to harmonize the mind, body, and spirit. By focusing on the

Merkaba symbol during therapy sessions, clients are encouraged to tap into their inner wisdom and healing capabilities. This approach often combines with other holistic methods like meditation, visualization, and breathing techniques to enhance the overall therapeutic experience. The goal is to foster a state of balance and well-being, where physical, emotional, and spiritual aspects are addressed cohesively.

Merkaba and Chakra Balancing

A significant aspect of Merkaba's use in modern healing revolves around chakra balancing. The Merkaba is believed to interact directly with the body's chakra system, unblocking and activating chakras to ensure a smooth flow of energy throughout the body. This practice is often incorporated into yoga and meditation sessions, where the visualization of the Merkaba aligns with the activation of each chakra, creating a powerful experience aimed at achieving inner harmony and heightened awareness.

Sound Healing and the Merkaba

Sound healing practitioners have found a unique ally in the Merkaba. Instruments like singing bowls, tuning forks, and pyramids are sometimes used in conjunction with the visualization of the Merkaba. The intersection of sound vibrations and the Merkaba's geometrical energy is believed to create a potent healing environment, facilitating deep relaxation and emotional release.

Merkaba in Mindfulness and Stress Reduction

In the context of mindfulness and stress reduction, Merkaba meditation offers a pathway to tranquility and mental clarity. Practitioners of this form of meditation focus on the Merkaba structure to achieve a state of deep relaxation, reducing stress and anxiety. The practice involves breathing techniques and guided visualizations, helping individuals to center themselves and find peace amidst the chaos of modern life.

Physical Health and Merkaba

Beyond its spiritual and emotional implications, Merkaba is also associated with physical health benefits. Some practitioners believe that meditating on the Merkaba symbol can boost the immune system, improve energy levels, and even aid in the healing of physical ailments. While these claims are largely anecdotal, they reflect the holistic nature of Merkaba's application in modern healing practices.

Merkaba in Personal Transformation

Merkaba is not only seen as a tool for healing but also as a catalyst for personal transformation. In various therapy and self-help groups, the principles of Merkaba are used to encourage personal growth, self-awareness, and emotional healing. Participants engage with the Merkaba concept to explore deeper aspects of their psyche, fostering growth and self-discovery.

Merkaba's Future in Healing Practices

As we look to the future, the role of Merkaba in healing practices seems poised for further exploration and innovation. The blend of ancient wisdom with modern healing techniques opens up new possibilities for health and well-being. Merkaba's potential in areas like virtual reality therapy, bioenergetics, and integrative medicine suggests an exciting trajectory, promising deeper insights and more effective healing modalities.

THE FUTURE OF MERKABA MYSTICISM

As we venture into the future of Merkaba mysticism within the framework of contemporary spirituality, we are poised at the cusp of a remarkable fusion of ancient wisdom and modern insights. Let's delve into the prospective pathways Merkaba might take as it continues to evolve and resonate with spiritual seekers worldwide.

Technological Integration in Merkaba Practices

The digital revolution offers new dimensions for Merkaba mysticism. Virtual reality (VR) and augmented reality (AR) technologies are beginning to find their way into spiritual practices, offering immersive experiences of Merkaba meditation. These technologies allow practitioners to visually and interactively explore the Merkaba's geometric structure, enhancing understanding and deepening the meditative experience. In the future, we might witness more sophisticated VR and AR applications designed to facilitate Merkaba journeys, making them more accessible and engaging.

Merkaba and Quantum Science

The intersection of Merkaba mysticism with quantum science is an area ripe for exploration. Quantum physics, with its focus on the fundamental nature of reality and consciousness, shares intriguing parallels with the principles of Merkaba. Future studies might delve deeper into how the Merkaba's geometric form relates to quantum theories of interconnectedness, energy fields, and the nature of the universe. This synergy could lead to a more profound scientific understanding of Merkaba and its role in the cosmic scheme.

Merkaba in Environmental and Social Activism

As global awareness of environmental and social issues grows, Merkaba mysticism could play a role in fostering a more harmonious relationship between humanity and the planet. Merkaba's principles of balance, interconnectedness, and transcendence might inspire environmental and social activists, guiding them towards more holistic and spiritually-informed approaches to activism. We could see Merkaba being used as a tool for raising consciousness about ecological balance, social harmony, and the interconnected nature of all life.

Personalized and Adaptive Merkaba Experiences

Advancements in AI and machine learning may enable the creation of personalized Merkaba experiences tailored to individual needs and spiritual paths. Such technologies could analyze an individual's unique energy patterns, emotional states, and spiritual inclinations, offering customized Merkaba meditations and practices. This personalization would make Merkaba mysticism more relevant and effective for a diverse range of practitioners.

Merkaba in Holistic Education

The potential of Merkaba mysticism in the realm of education is significant. Educators might increasingly incorporate Merkaba principles into curriculums, using its concepts to teach about geometry, history, spirituality, and personal development. This integration would offer students a more holistic understanding of the world, blending intellectual knowledge with spiritual wisdom.

Collaborative Merkaba Research and Practices

The future of Merkaba mysticism might also see increased collaboration between different spiritual traditions, scholars, and practitioners. Such collaborative efforts could lead to a richer, more diverse understanding of Merkaba, uncovering shared themes and practices across cultures. This collaborative approach would enhance the depth and reach of Merkaba mysticism, fostering a more inclusive and unified spiritual community.

Merkaba in Therapeutic Settings

The therapeutic potential of Merkaba is likely to be further explored. Mental health professionals could integrate Merkaba principles and practices into therapy sessions, using them as tools for emotional healing, self-discovery, and personal transformation. This integration would offer a more holistic approach to mental health, combining traditional therapeutic techniques with spiritual practices.

As we look to the future, Merkaba mysticism holds the promise of continued evolution and deeper integration into various aspects of human life. From technological advancements to social activism, education, and mental health, the potential applications of Merkaba are vast and varied. This journey into the future, grounded in ancient wisdom yet open to modern innovations, positions Merkaba as a key component in the ongoing quest for spiritual growth and understanding.

COMMUNITY
AND COLLECTIVE
CONSCIOUSNESS

BUILDING COMMUNITIES AROUND MERKABA

In the landscape of contemporary spirituality, Merkaba has emerged not only as a profound symbol of personal transformation but also as a catalyst for community building. Across the globe, individuals are drawn together by the shared interest in the mystical and transformative aspects of Merkaba, forming communities that transcend traditional boundaries.

Foundation of Merkaba Communities

Merkaba communities are often founded on principles of mutual support, spiritual exploration, and collective growth. They offer a space where individuals can explore the Merkaba's significance in meditation, healing, and personal evolution. These communities are diverse, including people from various cultural, religious, and social backgrounds, all united by their fascination with Merkaba's spiritual potential.

Role of Merkaba in Community Rituals and Ceremonies

Community rituals and ceremonies play a significant role in Merkaba practices. These gatherings often involve group meditations, energy work, and discussions on spiritual insights. Merkaba rituals are designed to enhance the collective energy of the group, facilitating deeper connections between participants and the universal energies represented by the Merkaba.

Merkaba Workshops and Retreats

Merkaba communities frequently organize workshops and retreats, offering immersive experiences in Merkaba practices. These events often feature guided meditations, teachings on sacred geometry, and exercises to activate the Merkaba field. These gatherings are not just learning experiences but also opportunities for community members to deepen their bonds and support each other's spiritual journeys.

Online Merkaba Communities

In the digital age, online platforms have become crucial in expanding Merkaba communities. Websites, forums, and social media groups enable individuals from all over the world to connect, share experiences, and learn from each other. Online communities provide accessibility to those who may not have local groups, fostering a global network of Merkaba practitioners.

Merkaba in Collaborative Art and Cultural Projects

Merkaba communities often engage in collaborative art and cultural projects. These projects range from creating Merkaba-inspired artworks to organizing cultural events that celebrate the spiritual significance of the Merkaba. Through these collaborative efforts, community members express their spiritual insights and contribute to a shared cultural identity centered around Merkaba.

Community Healing and Support

Healing and emotional support are integral to Merkaba communities. Members often come together to offer energy healing, emotional support, and spiritual guidance to each other. This collective approach to healing emphasizes the Merkaba's potential to harmonize and balance, not just at an individual level, but within a community context as well.

Merkaba in Environmental and Social Activism

Increasingly, Merkaba communities are involved in environmental and social activism. Inspired by the principles of interconnectedness and balance inherent in the Merkaba, these communities engage in activities aimed at promoting ecological sustainability, social justice, and global peace. This activism reflects the belief that spiritual awareness and social responsibility are deeply interconnected.

Future Prospects for Merkaba Communities

Looking to the future, Merkaba communities are likely to play an even more significant role in shaping the spiritual landscape. As interest in Merkaba mysticism grows, these communities will continue to evolve, potentially leading to new forms of spiritual expression and collective action.

MERKABA AND GLOBAL CONSCIOUSNESS

In the tapestry of global spirituality, the Merkaba symbol emerges as a pivotal element in the collective consciousness movement. Its geometric complexity and deep esoteric meanings have captured the imagination of spiritual communities worldwide, positioning it as a significant tool in the pursuit of a unified global consciousness.

Merkaba: A Universal Symbol of Interconnectedness

The Merkaba, often visualized as a three-dimensional Star of David, transcends cultural and religious boundaries, embodying a universal symbol of spiritual unity. It is seen as a representation of the macrocosm and microcosm, reflecting the interconnectedness of all life. This concept resonates deeply in the global consciousness movement, which emphasizes the interdependence of all beings and the collective responsibility towards the planet.

Role in Global Meditation and Healing Circles

Merkaba is frequently central to global meditation and healing circles. These gatherings, often synchronized across different time zones, aim to harness collective energy for planetary healing and consciousness elevation. Participants focus on the Merkaba to send out vibrations of peace, harmony, and healing, believing in the power of collective intention to bring about positive change in the world.

Merkaba in Consciousness Studies

Consciousness studies, exploring the nature of awareness and its connection to the universe, have begun to incorporate the Merkaba. Researchers in this field are interested in how Merkaba meditation affects the collective consciousness, potentially offering insights into the human

mind's capability to influence and be influenced by a collective energy field.

Influence on Art and Cultural Expressions

The Merkaba symbol has found its way into various forms of art and cultural expressions, serving as a motif that conveys messages of unity and spiritual awakening. Artists inspired by the Merkaba create works that evoke a sense of global citizenship and shared spiritual heritage, contributing to the collective consciousness movement.

Merkaba in Environmental Consciousness

Environmental movements have also adopted the Merkaba as a symbol of balance and sustainability. It is used to remind individuals of their connection to the earth and their responsibility towards environmental stewardship. In this context, the Merkaba symbolizes the delicate balance required to maintain ecological harmony and sustainability.

The Role of Technology in Spreading Merkaba Awareness

Advancements in technology have played a crucial role in spreading awareness of the Merkaba and its significance in global consciousness. Online platforms, social media, and virtual events have allowed for the sharing of knowledge, experiences, and Merkaba practices, reaching a global audience and fostering a sense of unity and shared purpose.

Merkaba in Education and Awareness Programs

Educational initiatives and awareness programs often incorporate the Merkaba to teach about global consciousness and interconnectedness. These programs aim to foster a sense of global community and responsibility, encouraging individuals to see themselves as part of a larger whole and to act in ways that benefit the planet and humanity.

Future Prospects in Global Consciousness Evolution

Looking ahead, the Merkaba's role in global consciousness is likely to expand and deepen. As humanity faces global challenges, the principles embodied by the Merkaba – interconnectedness, balance, and spiritual awakening – offer a hopeful path towards a more conscious and harmonious world.

MERKABA AS A TOOL FOR PEACE AND HARMONY

The Merkaba symbol, a sacred geometry shape made of two intersecting tetrahedrons, represents a powerful tool for spiritual growth and transformation. Used for centuries to access higher states of consciousness, the Merkaba symbolizes the union of spirit and body, surrounded by light. This ancient symbol is believed to activate the chakras and balance energies within the body, thereby promoting peace and harmony.

Merkaba in Meditation and Energy Healing

Merkaba plays a pivotal role in meditation practices. By focusing on the Merkaba symbol during meditation, individuals can align their energies, achieving a state of deep relaxation and inner peace. The visualization of the Merkaba serves as a focal point, aiding concentration and facilitating heightened awareness. This process can be especially effective in raising one's vibration, opening up to greater understanding and insight into their life journey.

Merkaba for Chakra Balancing

The Merkaba symbol is integral in chakra balancing practices. Each point of the star corresponds to one of the seven main chakras in the body. By visualizing or physically placing the

Merkaba near these energy centers, practitioners can restore balance and harmony to their chakras.

Merkaba as a Vehicle for Astral Travel

Some individuals use the Merkaba for astral travel or out-of-body experiences during deep meditation states. By activating their energetic field, they transcend physical limitations and explore higher realms.

Benefits of Working with a Merkaba

Working with a Merkaba can bring various benefits that positively impact life. It can enhance self-awareness, making individuals more attuned to their thoughts, emotions, and actions. This heightened self-awareness can lead to a deeper understanding of oneself and conscious choices aligned with true desires. Additionally, the Merkaba is believed to activate and align energy centers, including the third eye chakra associated with intuition, making intuitive abilities sharper and more reliable.

Merkaba for Healing and Protection

Many practitioners believe that the Merkaba can be harnessed for healing and protection. By visualizing the Merkaba around themselves or others, they access a powerful source of positive energy that can help restore balance and ward off negativity.

Merkaba and Sacred Geometry

Sacred geometry, which includes patterns like the Merkaba symbol, explores the hidden shapes that exist within nature, art, and architecture. These patterns are divinely inspired and have been used throughout history to create sacred spaces and objects. Understanding sacred geometry helps unravel the secrets behind the formation of a Merkaba and its symbolism.

Merkaba in Spiritual Enrichment and Retreats

The Merkaba symbol is also utilized in spiritual retreats, providing a peaceful environment for body and soul nurturing. Group and individual retreats often incorporate Merkaba meditation, aiding participants in their spiritual growth and transformation journeys.

Common Challenges in Merkaba Meditation

Practicing Merkaba meditation can be challenging initially, as the concept might seem complex. It's essential to maintain patience and seek guidance from experienced practitioners to overcome these challenges and debunk myths about Merkaba meditation.

Merkaba Meditation Techniques

Utilizing Merkaba in meditation involves visualization and breathing techniques. Practitioners visualize the Merkaba star and imagine it spinning, thereby tapping into its harmonic healing powers. This meditation can expand awareness, cleanse chakras, nurture intuitive elements of the brain, and reconnect with a deeper sense of self.

Merkaba, as a tool for peace and harmony, offers a pathway to spiritual growth, healing, and transformation. Its use in meditation, energy healing, and chakra balancing fosters inner peace, self-awareness, and a connection with the higher self. The Merkaba symbol's incorporation into modern spiritual practices continues to enrich the lives of those who engage with it.

CASE STUDIES AND EXPERIENCES

PERSONAL STORIES OF TRANSFORMATION THROUGH MERKABA PRACTICES

Journey of Spiritual Awakening

The journey into Merkaba spirituality often begins at a crossroads of personal crisis or a deep-seated yearning for meaning. For many, this journey has led to transformative experiences, marked by profound shifts in consciousness and an expanded understanding of the self and the universe. These narratives offer a window into the powerful impact of Merkaba in individuals' lives.

Healing and Emotional Rebirth

A common thread in these stories is the profound healing experienced through Merkaba practices. Individuals report overcoming deep-rooted emotional traumas, anxiety, and depression, attributing their healing to the energy work facilitated by Merkaba meditation. This healing often marks the beginning of a new chapter in their lives, characterized by greater emotional stability and clarity.

Discovering Inner Peace and Balance

Merkaba practices have led many to discover an inner peace and balance that transcends their everyday experiences. Practitioners describe this as a harmonizing of their inner and outer worlds, where stress and turmoil give way to a sense of calm and centeredness. This newfound balance is often cited as a turning point in their personal and professional lives.

Awakening to Higher Consciousness

A significant aspect of Merkaba's transformative power is the awakening to higher states of consciousness. Individuals recount experiences of profound insights, heightened intuition, and a deep connection with the universal energy. This awakening is described not as an escape from reality, but as an enriched engagement with it, filled with purpose and direction.

Integration into Daily Life

Transformation through Merkaba is not confined to the realms of meditation and spiritual practice. Many share how these principles have seamlessly integrated into their daily lives, influencing their relationships, career choices, and lifestyle. This integration reflects a holistic approach to spiritual growth, where the sacred geometry of Merkaba becomes a guiding symbol in everyday decisions.

Empowerment and Personal Growth

Engaging with Merkaba practices has empowered individuals to take charge of their life paths. Stories abound of people finding the courage to pursue their passions, make significant life changes, and embrace their authentic selves. This empowerment is often attributed to the clarity and self-awareness gained through Merkaba meditation.

Community and Shared Experiences

The collective aspect of Merkaba practices has fostered a sense of community and belonging among practitioners. Shared experiences in workshops, retreats, and online forums have created support networks where individuals encourage and inspire each other in their spiritual journeys. This sense of community is vital, providing a nurturing space for continued growth and exploration.

Transformative Impact on Physical Health

Beyond the psychological and spiritual benefits, Merkaba practices have also been linked to improvements in physical health. Participants report increased energy levels, improved immunity, and sometimes, alleviation of chronic physical ailments. These physical transformations further attest to the holistic nature of Merkaba as a tool for overall well-being.

The personal stories of transformation through Merkaba practices are as diverse as they are profound. They serve as testaments to the potential of ancient wisdom in modern times, offering hope, healing, and a path to a more conscious and fulfilling life.

MERKABA IN THERAPY AND COUNSELING - CASE STUDIES

Case Study 1: Alex's Journey Through Anxiety to Tranquility

Alex, a 30-year-old software developer, faced debilitating anxiety and panic attacks that hindered his daily activities and career progression. Despite trying various therapies and medications, the relief was temporary, and the root of his anxiety remained unaddressed. That's when his therapist introduced him to Merkaba meditation, a practice unfamiliar to Alex but one that would mark the beginning of a transformative journey.

Initially skeptical, Alex committed to a disciplined practice of guided Merkaba visualizations. He focused on visualizing the star tetrahedron surrounding him, spinning in harmonious opposite directions, embodying both masculine and feminine energy aspects. The visualization sessions, held twice weekly, were complemented by daily personal practice, fostering a deep connection with the Merkaba energy field.

Remarkably, within the first month, Alex reported a noticeable decrease in his anxiety levels. The panic attacks that once seemed imminent now rarely occurred. He found himself in a state of calmness previously unattainable, describing a newfound sense of being "centered" and "grounded." Over time, Alex's ability to manage stress improved significantly. He attributed this change to the Merkaba meditation, which not only provided him with a tool for immediate relief but also facilitated a deeper understanding of his inner world, allowing him to address the roots of his anxiety.

Case Study 2: Emma's Path to Healing Childhood Trauma

Emma, a 35-year-old teacher, carried the weight of childhood trauma into her adult life, manifesting as trust issues, emotional instability, and a pervasive sense of vulnerability. Traditional therapy sessions had offered some insights, but the emotional wounds remained open, affecting her relationships and self-esteem. Intrigued by the potential of incorporating spiritual practices into therapy, her counselor suggested Merkaba meditation as a complementary approach.

The therapy sessions began to include Merkaba-based visualizations, where Emma was guided to imagine herself within a Merkaba field, visualized as a vibrant, rotating star tetrahedron. This sacred geometry became a symbolic safe space for her, a protective field where she could confront and process her traumatic memories without fear.

As weeks turned into months, Emma experienced a profound shift in her emotional well-being. The Merkaba visualizations not only offered her a sense of safety and protection but also empowered her to view her past trauma from a place of strength and resilience. She reported a significant reduction in her feelings of vulnerability, and for the first time in years, she felt a genuine sense of healing and emotional liberation.

These sessions, integrating the principles of Merkaba, transformed Emma's therapeutic journey, enabling her to heal from her trauma in a way that traditional therapy alone had not facilitated. The practice provided her with both a metaphorical and a tangible framework for rebuilding her emotional foundation, leading to lasting improvements in her personal and professional life.

Case Study 3: Reconnecting Julia and Michael Through Merkaba

Julia and Michael, both in their late thirties, reached a critical point in their marriage where ongoing communication breakdowns threatened their relationship. Despite their deep love for each other, misunderstandings and unexpressed feelings had created a barrier they couldn't seem to overcome. In search of a non-traditional approach to mend their relationship, they were introduced to a therapist specializing in Merkaba for couples counseling.

In their sessions, the therapist introduced the concept of Merkaba, emphasizing its symbolism of interconnectedness, balance, and the union of opposing energies. Julia and Michael engaged in joint meditation sessions, focusing on visualizing a shared Merkaba field surrounding them. This practice was aimed at not only individual healing and understanding but also at nurturing the space between them, filled with shared energy and intentions.

Through these sessions, Julia and Michael began to experience a shift in their relationship. The Merkaba meditations served as a powerful metaphor for their partnership, illustrating how two individuals could come together, creating something greater than themselves. They reported a newfound appreciation for each other's perspectives, leading to deeper empathy and significantly improved communication.

The couple's journey through Merkaba-based counseling transformed their approach to conflicts and misunderstandings. By focusing on their shared energy field and intentions, they learned to navigate their differences with love and respect, revitalizing the connection that had brought them together.

Case Study 4: Lucas's Path Out of Depression with Merkaba Energy Work

Lucas, a 28-year-old graphic designer, had been battling depression for several years. Traditional therapy and medication had provided some relief, but Lucas sought a more holistic approach to address the root of his emotional pain. Intrigued by the concept of energy work, he began therapy sessions focused on Merkaba energy work.

The therapist guided Lucas through the process of activating his Merkaba field, focusing on breathwork, visualization, and intention-setting. The sessions aimed to balance Lucas's emotional state, clearing blockages that contributed to his depression. By visualizing the Merkaba field spinning around him, Lucas learned to channel universal energy for healing and balance.

Over several months of consistent practice, Lucas noticed a profound change in his emotional well-being. The depressive episodes that once clouded his days became less frequent and less intense. He reported feeling a sense of liberation from the weight of his depression, describing an overall lift in mood and a burgeoning sense of spiritual awakening.

Lucas's journey with Merkaba energy work opened a new chapter in his life. He found a source of inner strength and balance that had been missing in his battle with depression. This holistic approach provided him not only with symptomatic relief but also with a deeper connection to his spiritual self, offering a sense of peace and emotional resilience that he had long sought.

Case Study 5: Emily's Breakthrough in Self-Discovery

Emily, a 29-year-old marketing executive, found herself at a crossroads in her career and personal life. Despite her external success, she felt unfulfilled and disconnected from her true self. Seeking deeper meaning and direction, Emily turned to a therapist who specialized in integrating Merkaba meditation into personal development practices.

During her therapy sessions, Emily was introduced to the principles of Merkaba meditation. She learned to visualize the geometric energy field around her, focusing on its rotation to tap into higher states of consciousness. This practice became a daily ritual, providing her with a profound sense of peace and clarity.

As Emily delved deeper into her Merkaba practice, she began to uncover insights about her life path that had previously eluded her. She realized that her career, while successful on the surface, did not align with her core values and passions. Similarly, reflections on her personal relationships revealed patterns that stifled her growth and happiness.

The most significant breakthrough came when Emily identified her true calling—using her marketing skills for social impact. She also recognized the importance of nurturing relationships that supported her growth. This clarity empowered Emily to make bold decisions: transitioning her career towards social entrepreneurship and redefining her personal boundaries and connections.

Emily's journey through Merkaba meditation marked a pivotal point in her life. The practice not only facilitated a deep connection with her inner self but also provided the courage and clarity to align her external world with her newfound inner truth.

Case Study 6: Collective Transformation in Group Therapy

A diverse group of individuals, ranging from their late twenties to mid-forties, participated in a unique group therapy session centered around Merkaba meditation. Facilitated by a therapist experienced in energy work, the group sessions were designed to foster a sense of community and shared healing.

The group met weekly, sitting in a circle to enhance the collective energy flow. They were guided through Merkaba visualizations, focusing on creating and maintaining a unified energy field around the group. Participants were encouraged to set personal intentions, while also contributing to a collective intention for healing and growth.

As the weeks progressed, the group dynamic began to deeply influence the individual and collective experiences. Participants reported feeling a profound connection with one another, transcending their initial feelings of isolation. The shared Merkaba field became a powerful catalyst for healing, amplifying the energy work and facilitating experiences of unity and empathy.

One remarkable outcome of these sessions was the spontaneous emergence of a support network within the group. Members shared personal challenges and breakthroughs, offering each other empathy, insight, and encouragement. This sense of belonging and mutual support led to significant personal transformations, with individuals reporting marked improvements in their emotional well-being, relationships, and self-perception.

The group therapy case highlighted Merkaba's potential to create a supportive community environment conducive to healing. The collective energy work not only enhanced individual journeys of growth but also fostered a powerful sense of unity and shared purpose among the participants.

Case Study 7: Marcus's Journey to Enhanced Mindfulness

Marcus, a 34-year-old architect, had been practicing mindfulness meditation for several years as a way to manage the pressures of his demanding career. While he found these practices beneficial, he sought a deeper level of focus and presence. His journey led him to a workshop on Merkaba techniques, where he hoped to find the enrichment he was looking for.

The workshop introduced Marcus to the concept of the Merkaba field—a geometric energy form surrounding the body, which can be activated through specific visualizations and breathwork. Integrating these Merkaba techniques into his daily meditation routine, Marcus embarked on a new phase of his mindfulness journey.

Over the following months, Marcus noticed a significant enhancement in his meditation experience. The Merkaba visualizations helped him achieve a state of focus and presence he had not previously attained. He reported experiencing moments of profound clarity and connection, both with himself and the world around him.

This deepened mindfulness practice began to reflect in Marcus's daily life. He found himself more engaged in his work, approaching architectural challenges with a newfound creativity and calmness. His interactions with colleagues and clients became more thoughtful and compassionate, leading to more meaningful professional relationships.

Marcus's exploration of Merkaba techniques not only enriched his mindfulness practice but also transformed his approach to life and work. He became an advocate for integrating Merkaba into mindfulness practices, sharing his experiences with others seeking a deeper connection with the present moment.

Case Study 8: A Corporate Shift Towards Calmness with Merkaba

A tech startup, recognizing the high stress levels among its employees, initiated a corporate wellness program that included a series of workshops on stress management. One of these workshops focused on Merkaba meditation techniques, designed to offer employees tools for managing stress in a novel and effective way.

The workshop, led by a certified Merkaba practitioner, introduced employees to the basics of Merkaba meditation, including breathwork and visualization of the tetrahedral energy field. Skeptical at first, participants soon began to experience the benefits of the practice, dedicating a few minutes each day to Merkaba meditation.

Feedback collected over the next few months highlighted remarkable changes within the workforce. Employees reported feeling significantly less stressed, noting a marked improvement in their ability to handle the fast-paced and often unpredictable nature of their work. Many cited experiencing a greater sense of clarity and calmness, not just in the workplace but in their personal lives as well.

Managers observed a shift in the company culture, with teams displaying improved collaboration and communication. The overall work environment became more positive, with a noticeable decrease in absenteeism and employee burnout.

The success of the Merkaba workshop in this corporate

setting underscored the versatility and effectiveness of Merkaba techniques for stress management. The company continued to integrate Merkaba practices into its wellness program, setting a precedent for holistic employee care in the corporate world.

These case studies demonstrate the versatility and effectiveness of Merkaba in various therapeutic settings. From personal healing to relationship counseling, Merkaba's principles offer a unique approach to mental and emotional well-being.

MERKABA IN EDUCATIONAL SETTINGS

Incorporating Merkaba in Classroom Learning

Merkaba has found its way into educational settings as an innovative tool to enhance learning experiences. Teachers have begun integrating Merkaba principles to foster a holistic learning environment. This includes using Merkaba geometry as a teaching aid in subjects like mathematics and art, helping students to understand complex geometrical concepts and explore creativity.

Merkaba for Student Well-being and Mindfulness

Schools and universities are increasingly recognizing the importance of student well-being. Merkaba meditation and mindfulness practices are being incorporated into the curriculum to help students manage stress and anxiety. These practices are not only improving students' mental health but also enhancing their concentration and learning abilities.

Merkaba in Special Education

In special education, Merkaba has been used as a therapeutic tool to assist students with learning disabilities and emotional challenges. Educators report that Merkaba's visual and meditative techniques help in improving focus, emotional regulation, and self-expression among these students.

Enhancing Creativity and Critical Thinking

Merkaba's sacred geometry is being employed as a basis for creative and critical thinking exercises. Students are encouraged to explore Merkaba patterns, leading to deeper engagement with mathematical concepts and development of problem-solving skills. This approach fosters an environment where learning is not just about memorization, but understanding and application.

Teacher Training and Professional Development

Educational institutions are also focusing on teacher training programs that incorporate Merkaba principles. These programs aim to equip educators with tools to create a more engaging, mindful, and supportive learning environment. Teachers trained in Merkaba techniques are better prepared to address diverse learning needs and foster a positive educational atmosphere.

Merkaba in Cultural and Historical Education

Merkaba is being used as a gateway to explore various cultural and historical contexts in the classroom. Through the study of Merkaba, students gain insights into different spiritual and philosophical traditions, enhancing their global awareness and appreciation for cultural diversity.

Merkaba and Environmental Education

Some educators have linked Merkaba principles to environmental education, emphasizing the connection between sacred geometry, nature, and sustainability. This approach encourages students to see the interdependence between themselves and the natural world, promoting environmental stewardship.

Technology-Enhanced Learning with Merkaba

Advancements in technology have enabled the integration of Merkaba into digital learning platforms. Interactive software and virtual reality experiences are being developed to provide immersive learning experiences, where students can explore the three-dimensional aspects of Merkaba geometry in a virtual space.

Impact on Social and Emotional Learning

Merkaba's role in promoting social and emotional learning (SEL) is noteworthy. By incorporating these practices, students develop key skills such as empathy, emotional intelligence, and social awareness. This holistic approach to education is preparing students not just academically, but also for their emotional and social lives.

The use of Merkaba in educational settings represents a shift towards a more integrated approach to learning. It combines intellectual, emotional, and spiritual development, preparing students for a well-rounded life both within and beyond the classroom.

CONCLUSIONS
AND FURTHER
EXPLORATION

SUMMARIZING
MERKABA'S ESSENCE

The Concept of Merkaba

Merkaba, a term rooted in ancient Hebrew, translates to 'light', 'spirit', and 'body'. This concept represents a field of divine energy that is believed to surround and penetrate the human body. At its core, Merkaba is a symbol of metaphysical balance and cosmic harmony, illustrating the interconnectedness of the physical and spiritual realms.

Merkaba's Geometrical Structure

The Merkaba is visualized as a star tetrahedron, consisting of two interlocking tetrahedra pointing in opposite directions. This geometry is not just a static symbol but is perceived as a dynamic, spinning field that radiates energy. The intersecting tetrahedra symbolize the duality of existence — spirit and matter, male and female, earth and cosmos — merging to create a harmonious whole.

Merkaba and Sacred Geometry

Merkaba is a key figure in sacred geometry, a field that attributes symbolic and sacred meanings to certain geometric shapes. It's considered a powerful tool for spiritual growth, serving as a vehicle for traveling between dimensions and accessing higher levels of consciousness.

Merkaba in Spiritual and Meditation Practices

In spiritual practices, particularly in meditation, Merkaba is used as a focal point for accessing higher states of consciousness. It is believed to aid in spiritual awakening and enlightenment. Practitioners often visualize the Merkaba surrounding them, spinning in opposite directions, to align their energy fields and connect with higher dimensions.

Merkaba's Healing Properties

Merkaba is also associated with healing. It is believed to harmonize and balance the energy fields around the body, aiding in physical, emotional, and spiritual healing. By aligning the spiritual and physical bodies, Merkaba helps in clearing energy blockages and restoring balance.

The Symbolism of Merkaba

As a symbol, Merkaba represents the concept of 'as above, so below', indicating the link between the earthly and spiritual realms. It embodies the idea that the microcosm reflects the macrocosm and vice versa. This symbolism is integral in understanding the interconnectedness of all things in the universe.

Merkaba's Historical and Cultural Significance

Throughout history, Merkaba has been revered in various cultures and spiritual traditions. In Jewish mysticism, particularly in Kabbalah, it's linked to the chariot of God and spiritual ascension. The symbol has also been found in ancient Egyptian texts, where it is associated with the process of spiritual enlightenment.

Merkaba in Modern Context

In contemporary spirituality, Merkaba has been adopted as a tool for personal and collective transformation. It's seen as a key to unlocking deeper understanding of oneself and the universe, and for navigating the journey of spiritual growth and self-discovery.

Merkaba's Future Prospects

As spiritual awareness continues to evolve, Merkaba's role in facilitating a deeper connection with the divine is likely to gain more recognition. Its principles are increasingly being integrated into various healing and mindfulness practices, indicating a growing acknowledgment of its transformative potential.

CHALLENGES AND CONTROVERSIES IN MERKABA PRACTICE

Criticisms of Cognitive Limitations

Merkaba, while revered in spiritual circles, faces criticisms regarding its cognitive implications. Critics argue that focusing solely on symbols like Merkaba, especially in complex systems such as spirituality, can lead to cognitive reductionism. This reductionism may oversimplify the multifaceted nature of human consciousness and spiritual experiences, potentially leading to misleading interpretations and practices.

Misconceptions about Merkaba Meditation

Merkaba meditation, often associated with energy fields and consciousness ascension, is sometimes misunderstood as a religious practice confined to specific belief systems. This misconception overlooks its universal nature and the diverse cultural backgrounds from which it derives. Merkaba's widespread interpretation across various cultures and traditions is sometimes lost in contemporary practices, leading to a narrowed understanding of its essence.

Overemphasis on Symbolism

While the use of symbols is integral to Merkaba practice, there is a debate over the extent to which symbolism should dominate spiritual practices. The overemphasis on Merkaba's geometrical and symbolic aspects may detract from its deeper spiritual meanings and applications. This overemphasis can potentially reduce Merkaba to a mere icon, rather than a tool for profound spiritual exploration and transformation.

Challenges in Integrating Ancient Wisdom with Modern Practices

The integration of ancient Merkaba principles into modern spiritual practices presents challenges. The original contexts and understandings of Merkaba in ancient texts and traditions are sometimes lost or altered when adapted to contemporary settings. This gap between traditional wisdom and modern interpretation can lead to misapplications and misunderstandings of Merkaba's true essence.

Controversy in Kabbalistic Interpretations

In Kabbalistic studies, texts like the Sefer Yetzirah, which delve into Merkaba mysticism, are subject to controversy. Debates exist over the classification of these texts due to their early composition dates and potential gnostic influences. The complexity of these texts adds to the challenge of accurately interpreting and applying their teachings in the context of Merkaba.

Commercialization and Misrepresentation

The commercialization of Merkaba, particularly in the form of jewelry, talismans, and meditation aids, has raised concerns about the misrepresentation of its sacredness. The marketing of Merkaba-themed products can sometimes trivialize its spiritual significance, reducing it to a commodity rather than a revered symbol of spiritual enlightenment.

Potential for Misuse in Rituals

Merkaba's use in rituals, whether individually or in groups, requires a deep understanding and respect for its spiritual significance. There is a risk of misuse or misinterpretation, especially when participants are not fully aware or aligned with the ritual's intent. Proper guidance and knowledge are crucial to ensure that Merkaba rituals are conducted with the reverence and understanding they deserve.

Varied Experiences and Skepticism

Individual experiences with Merkaba meditation and practice vary widely, leading to skepticism about its effectiveness. While some practitioners report profound spiritual transformations, others may not experience any significant changes, contributing to doubts about Merkaba's universal applicability and efficacy.

Merkaba's journey through sacred geometry and spiritual awakening is not without its challenges and controversies. From cognitive limitations and misconceptions to the difficulties of integrating ancient wisdom in modern times, these issues highlight the need for a nuanced and respectful approach to Merkaba practice.

CONTINUING THE MERKABA JOURNEY

Evolving Understanding of Merkaba

As spirituality evolves, the understanding and practice of Merkaba continue to expand. The journey with Merkaba is not static; it grows and changes with time, accommodating new insights from various spiritual and scientific perspectives. This evolution encourages practitioners to continuously explore and deepen their relationship with Merkaba.

Advanced Merkaba Meditation Techniques

Merkaba meditation, central to Merkaba practice, advances beyond basic visualizations to more complex techniques. These advanced methods involve intricate breathwork patterns, specific hand placements (mudras), and focused intentions. These practices are designed to enhance the practitioner's experience of spiritual ascension and consciousness expansion.

Integration of Merkaba into Various Spiritual Practices

Merkaba's principles are being integrated into diverse spiritual practices beyond traditional meditation. This includes its use in energy healing, astral travel, and even in rituals and ceremonies. Each practice offers a unique pathway to experiencing and harnessing the energy of Merkaba.

The Merkaba and Personal Transformation

Continuing the journey with Merkaba involves using it as a tool for personal transformation. This includes self-reflection, overcoming personal challenges, and aligning with one's higher self. The Merkaba becomes a symbol and instrument for profound personal growth and understanding.

Merkaba in Community and Collective Consciousness

The communal aspect of Merkaba practice is gaining prominence. Building communities around Merkaba practices fosters a collective consciousness that transcends individual experiences. These communities provide support, share insights, and contribute to a shared journey of spiritual evolution.

Merkaba in Contemporary Healing Practices

The integration of Merkaba into modern healing modalities continues to evolve. From energy healing to therapy and counseling, Merkaba's principles are being adapted to suit contemporary needs, offering holistic healing that encompasses mind, body, and spirit.

The Future of Merkaba Mysticism

The journey with Merkaba is also a journey into its future potential. Speculation and exploration into the future directions of Merkaba practice are encouraged. This includes potential new discoveries in the fields of quantum physics, neuroscience, and the study of consciousness, which may shed new light on Merkaba's ancient wisdom.

Exploring Merkaba's Global and Cultural Perspectives

The global and cultural dimensions of Merkaba are expanding, with practitioners exploring how different cultures and spiritual traditions understand and use Merkaba. This exploration enriches the practice by bringing in diverse perspectives and deepening the collective understanding of Merkaba's role in spirituality.

Continuing Education and Research

The Merkaba journey involves ongoing education and research. Practitioners are encouraged to engage with new studies, attend workshops, and connect with experts in the field. This continuous learning ensures that the practice remains vibrant, relevant, and informed by the latest insights.

Personal Journey with Merkaba

Ultimately, the journey with Merkaba is a deeply personal one. Each practitioner is encouraged to find their own path with Merkaba, exploring its significance and application in their own life. This personal exploration is what makes the journey with Merkaba a lifelong and ever-evolving process.

Thank you for sharing in this exploration of the mysteries of Merkaba. I wish you happiness and enlightenment in your own journey.

THE END

Printed in Great Britain
by Amazon

62799638R00087